With many thanks to my dear friend
Dame Virginia McKenna OBE actress, author,
tireless wildlife campaigner and co-founder
of the Born Free Foundation for her
encouraging words and help regarding this book.
Also thanks to friends from my Writing Group:
Patti, Christine, Julia, Jan, David and Sylvia,
for 'listening' and for their invaluable feed-back.

The Boy from the Salt Marsh

Books by the same author:

2 Steps Behind …

A Bear called Basher

Magnus, Aye-Aye and the
Flying Saucer

Running with Wolves

The Princess and the Chimney Sweep

Burnt Toast

The Elephants Mirror

The Curse of the Sea Witch

Another Place Another Time

The Boy from the Saltmarsh

Dawn Lawrence

Illustrations Dawn Lawrence

Published by
Aldabra Publishing
'Five Wishes' Jarvis Close
Stalbridge, Dorset
DT10 2PQ

Text Dawn Lawrence 2020
Illustrations Dawn Lawrence 2020

First Published 2020
by Aldabra Publishing
'Five Wishes', Stalbridge, Dorset DT10 2PQ

Printed in Great Britain by

Unit 4, Barton View business Park, Sheeplands Lane
Sherborne, Dorset
DT9 4FW

ISBN 978-1-9162035-2-5

To Kevin

Who shares with me the magic of words

"Is it real? Or an illusion? Can a boy really change from human to non-human? This is a mystery story with a difference – told by a wonderful story-teller, and for me, one I couldn't put down.

The strange, fascinating and, sometimes, other-worldly adventures of Morgan and her brother Kyle, will leave you no choice but to follow them. And, when you come to the final page, you know that it is not really the end."

Dame Virginia McKenna OBE
Co-Founder and Trustee
The Born Free Foundation

Slide through the surf, slip through the swell,
Hear the sound of a lost church bell;
Leave the marshes and follow the waves
Down, fathoms down, to the kind sea caves;
There's none that venture will be so rich
As those that embrace the wild Sea Witch

The Boy from the Salt Marsh

1

We did lots of things like other youngsters in those far off days. We lived on Salt Marsh Way on the coastal road at the end of which lay the lonely and mysterious marshes. We were guided by the old folk who knew all the safe footpaths but nowadays visitors who trek across take maps or follow signposts in order to steer clear of the treacherous parts.

It was all saltmarsh between us and the sea; mile after mile of it. The town stood on the first rising ground. At certain times when the moon was brightest one could imagine it was all water and the sea had drowned the land.

We went to St. Peter's School overlooking the harbour which was built for the fishing community; a poor school and a rough one. Although we came from a coastguard family we didn't mix with the fisher folk. All their rows of little cottages had steep steps leading down to the sea with small yards strung out with wash - washing lines. If we got up early enough on a week-end, my young brother and I would run down to the harbour just in time to see the first catch arrive at the market where the fish were sold from barrows.

There were just the two of us, brother and sister. My name being Morgan was deemed unusual for a girl, but it reminded me of the legendary Morgan le Fay, sister of the famous King Arthur who was also a sorceress. Kyle is my brother, a few years younger than me.

But then we met up with Finn, and our lives changed forever.

'He ran away from home, didn't he?' Kyle asked one day.

And I said 'Hush … mustn't talk about it. He told me that his dad made him work so hard and was so bad to him, he just up and left and never went back. The police were out looking for him for over a year. They couldn't find him.'

'But *we* did,' Kyle replied smugly.

It was true. One day we took a journey on a different route to the ones we were usually familiar with, and came across a wooden cabin raised on stilted legs, the home of an old toothless woman who smoked a clay pipe. She had wrinkled yellow skin and long white hair. Her eyes, though, stopped you in your tracks. They were quick and small, piercing like a ferret's, and dark with secrets. We'd never met anyone like her before and learnt that she was over a hundred years old. She was Finn's grandmother. He took shelter with her, and all the magic he possessed he learnt from her.

Finn himself was tall and wiry, with arms and legs which didn't look as though they belonged to him. He had striking red hair, green eyes, freckles, and a mouth creased into a perpetual grin. He told us that his colouring came from his Irish ancestors but we never knew if he was joking. He was much older than us, but quite how much older we never liked to ask. We didn't tell him a lot about ourselves. We didn't have to. Finn seemed to know everything about everyone. He was certainly not surprised at the news that our widowed father had taken up with another woman and left as soon as he reckoned I was old enough to take care of Kyle. School was no obstacle. Kyle played truant so often, using one excuse after another, he was hardly missed and we were soon left to make our own way in the world. This involved picking up odd jobs wherever possible, and our situation soon attracted sympathy and help from our small local community. "Those little gypsy kids" they called us.

I suppose we were always easy to identify even when there was a crowd at the summer fairs: the small, brown skinned, rather too slender girl, with dark shoulder-length hair dressed in an odd variety of clothes always accompanied by her young brother with his unkempt blond curls, taller than her, but shy, always keeping close at her heels with trousers and shirts several sizes too big for his skinny frame; a couple of misfits.

Occasionally I would still hear echoes of my father's warning to us before he left home. "Remember … don't mess with that lot on the marshes; rough, low, ignorant folk they are."

But Finn was different, different beyond our wildest dreams.

2

We stayed with Finn in his grandmother's cabin, which was deceivingly more spacious than one would imagine. There wasn't much room for the four of us, but Kyle and I slept in rough bunk beds built beneath a wall cupboard in one corner. It was a bleak place where the wind whistled as if calling … crying … always trying to find a way in; a place where on most days everything merged into a clinging grey mist so you could barely see where the sea ended and the land began.

Finn's grandmother didn't bother us, she just watched us warily at times with her black button eyes and went about her daily routine of fishing for eels and sea crabs along the shoreline.

Finn explained how he had promised to look after that stretch of land on which his grand-father had built the cabin years ago. There were a few plans he wanted to test. And we helped him to work with nature making a structure from scrub, stones and mud to trap sediment. He wanted to see if it would work on a small scale. Otherwise he would try another way, he told us.

'What way is that?' I asked. And he explained that he had a plan to create small ponds allowing some of the water to flow in.

'That might be a better idea,' Kyle agreed. But once he had me on my own, he pulled a face, and said it wouldn't work trying to save the land from the sea, the sea would always win.

And I tried to find a compromise. 'It might last until he thinks of something else. It's rumoured that Finn does things in mysterious ways.'

They were ways we had yet to discover of course. But he must have known what we were talking about, for later on he tried to explain. 'I would rather work *with* the sea than against it.' And I knew he was thinking of the sinister side of it, which he named the Sea Witch. It was all part of the amazing relationship he had forged with the elements: the wind, the sky, the land and sea. All held a special energy and force he could draw upon.

So after we completed one traditional course of thinking without much success we tried another. And once the water found its level it stood in dark pools of inky blackness, shining, and looking somehow ominous. Or so it appeared to me, which I thought rather strange since it was only water.

But I saw what Finn meant when he said that rising sea levels were water logging the marsh, killing off the vegetation as they retreated backwards, and that the marshes acted as a buffer protecting against storms by absorbing rainwater.

'Think of wind blowing through a forest,' he said. Plants reduce the energy of the water as it flows through and around them; a clever idea.'

We had to agree with him and looked rather subdued.

Finn gave one of his lopsided grins. 'But sometimes the Sea Witch helps instead of threatens,' he added. 'She sends in strong winds and tides and waves, and mixes sand and seaweeds. On some beaches there are fossilized forests many thousands of years old which she has uncovered from a time when man went hunting and gathering where you can still see remains of creatures that roamed there. Even foot prints of adults and children have been discovered.'

'But don't worry,' Finn laughed. 'I'm salt marsh by nature,' 'I can absorb more and still carry on.'

3

Before we had been with him very long, we experienced our first adventure. It was when he showed us a long pipe he had made from some reeds. There was nothing remarkable about it, being rather crudely made I thought. However his next words caused me to feel a ripple of excitement.

'I will play for you, and you will tell me afterwards what comes after. If it sends you to sleep, I warn you, don't be surprised if you find yourselves in quite another place and time; the elements of nature play tricks - and danger lurks in the water. The Sea Witch has her own magic.'

So he played for us … and the spell began. It was slow and sensual. But it wasn't a recognizable tune; just a string of soft, wild notes that held one in thrall.

In a very few moments we began to feel its effects, and I took one quick glance at Kyle who had already begun to close his eyes. Speaking for myself I fell almost at once into a deep sleep. It was as if I stepped from one dimension into another. But all the while I was aware of Kyle being at my side.

We were on the banks of a wide river. There was nothing to tell which country or part of it we were in, and I was about to mention this to Kyle, when a movement caught my eye accompanied by a thudding sound.

Turning round a little, I was astonished to see a horse trotting along the bank towards us. The animal was slender of build with an arch to its neck and a coat which seemed to glow in the sun with the touch of gold. As we continued to watch, it stopped and looked towards us. But it did not falter; there was no fear about it, only what I assumed was curiosity. And then it came within a few paces of us and, lowering its head, began to drink at the river's edge.

I motioned my intention to Kyle, and he followed close behind me as I ventured closer to the creature. Raising its head it eyed us warily before retreating a few steps. Somehow, involuntarily, I had the feeling that although wild now, it once had a rider and was therefore not afraid of us.

Gradually, patiently, I sidled up to it and offered my outstretched hand. The creature snorted and stamped its foot, but then accepted my gesture, blowing gently through my fingers. I ran my hands along its withers and across its back, admiring its thick mane and fine tail.

I had ridden horses before and Kyle also was used to them, so it was only a matter of time before I gained the animal's confidence enough to mount him. I gave Kyle a hand up, and once seated behind me, we began to trot and then to canter along the river bank.

It was exhilarating … just the three of us off to goodness knows where! I twined my fingers through the flowing mane, and closed my eyes against the wind. The horse ran faster, almost effortlessly, and I felt Kyle at my back egging us on.

And then quite suddenly all changed and I became aware that I was no longer controlling the horse, that *it* was controlling *me*. I had never gained mastery over a free running horse, and no matter how I exerted my will, there was no response. So there seemed no point in trying to contact its mind. The animal was not at all the one I had envisaged; it was quite a different creature.

Where would it take us? I was sure now that my own folly had led us astray, and that we were under some kind of enchantment.

And then the thought that had nudged me at the back of my mind came to the forefront; something I had dreaded and thrust aside. What if the animal decided to cross the river? It was wide, it was deep, and I had Kyle clinging at my back. I remembered that in all the dreams I had in the past, if I dared to anticipate a thing, it would come to pass. This time was no exception.

My mount was moving towards the landward side when it suddenly changed direction and turned in towards the river. In a few moments we had entered the water, and I held my breath. I turned my head into the screaming wind that had arisen, trying to shield my face as we plunged in and went deeper.

The water soon began to come over the horse's back and I saw that we had left the land far behind. Presently I became aware that the freshwater had turned to salt as we approached the mouth of the estuary, and that we had been carried out to sea.

I tried to cry out to Kyle, but my voice was carried away on the wind. We held on tightly although we gasped for breath and the salt water flooded our eyes, nose and mouth. The horse's breathing became erratic, loud and laboured, and its head went under at last and I knew it was fighting for its life. The end came quickly. It sank beneath us and the current carried it away.

I heard Kyle shouting for me, and I took a long breath battling my way towards him. I managed to grab and hold on to him, but it was difficult to keep our heads above water. We had to surface, gasping for air. I tried not to panic, but I knew it was hopeless and that very soon we would follow the same fate as the horse. At the same time I became aware of a force coursing through the waves – something I had no answer for - pulling us down with a grasping motion that emanated from somewhere far below.

And then it happened – almost like a dream. A giant dolphin came into view, rising out from the waves quite close to us. I gasped, and swallowed a mouthful of seawater.

It whistled loudly; then to our great astonishment it swam up to us and gently butted us with its head. We understood its intention at once, since it began to push and propel us along until we were out of dangerous deep water. The moment we were close enough to shore, it turned and headed back to sea.

Coughing up seawater and trembling from cold and the shock of our ordeal, we scrambled ashore, hardly able to believe that we had survived - and in such a miraculous way.

But we had an even greater surprise later, when we related our adventure to Finn. He was at once familiar with all that had happened.

'I thought when you became drowsy so quickly after my little musical performance that it seemed suspicious. There are powers and forces which one cannot always comprehend, living on land.'

I gasped. 'On *land* … You mean the Sea Witch had something to do with it?'

'She had everything to do with it,' Finn exclaimed. 'Did you not feel her force?'

I shivered. 'Yes, I remember now – there *was*

something – like a strong current pulling us down.'

'And the dolphin?' Kyle asked. 'What about the dolphin?'

'Ah, that was me, I'm afraid. Not a true dolphin in the sense of the word.'

We couldn't believe our ears, and Finn was obliged to explain that he was someone with this special ability to shapeshift; one who could create illusions. 'It has some- thing to do with the time I was born, when the earth passes into a certain phase and messes up time as we know it.'

But Kyle was not satisfied with this, as I thought he would not be. So he pressed Finn to answer more questions.

'Can you do this at any time? And can other people do it?'

'Only if the need is great I do it; if there is no other way or when a strong dream catches me. It has to act and behave as I wish. And it's not just peculiar to *me*; many others do it, but one just doesn't bump into them that often. People round here - the locals - say it has strong links with death and rebirth.'

'Wow!' Kyle exclaimed, and I shook my head

in disbelief. But Finn ended by saying that the phenomenon had been around since the beginning of time, and it might be that people had just forgotten how to do it. Meditation was one way, he said, but there were other ways.

'And the dolphin was really *you* all the time,' Kyle persisted, as if he was obliged to hammer the thought somehow into his head.

'It was an energy force necessary for survival. I had to find a way—and quickly—to save you from what I felt the Sea Witch might do once she had you where she wanted you.'

However there was one other thing that puzzled me which we had not touched upon, and that was the subject of dreams and dreaming. So I asked Finn about mutual dreaming, if this was in fact possible. And he told me that two people *could* meet and share the same dream. So that was something I was better able to understand, and that part of it at least was true.

I thought I would never sleep that night. Everything was so strange and exciting. But the next day the most unexpected and horrific thing happened.

Kyle disappeared

4

We didn't miss him at first. We just thought he'd got up early in the morning before us and wandered off somewhere as he often did. He liked to see the sun coming up over the horizon flooding the marsh with golden pools of light. But he always returned for breakfast and, when he didn't, we knew something was wrong.

Finn and I set out straight away to search for him. Finn knew the signs to look for, and judged the way he must have gone. But after we had travelled some distance, he stopped and shook his head. He had lost the trail.

He rubbed his head thoughtfully whilst I waited; wondering what was to come next. Then he murmured a few indistinct words to himself and scratched some marks on a patch of mud at his feet. As I watched he drew out some stones from his jacket pocket and cast them in what seemed to be a careless motion to land on the ground beside him. When I asked what these were, he said they were rune stones, and in fact I did afterwards discover some strange inscriptions incised upon each.

We then followed a new track and trod a path where the footing was treacherous and the swampy terrain gurgled and squelched as we walked. Finn had to feel his way carefully whilst I followed closely behind. Our progress was slow and exhausting until we left the marsh behind us and arrived some miles further along the coast at a small jetty. Beside it was a large shed used as a storage place for the various lobster pots, fishing nets and lines, and other tackle used by the local fisher folk.

The sound of voices came from within, and Finn grabbed my arm and motioned me to keep quiet. There were one or two windows set in the sides of the building which afforded us a good enough view of the interior.

A rough looking man was seated on a barrel, in front of which stood Kyle. There were two other men besides, and all were talking to him in an agitated way which involved much hand waving. They were obviously asking him questions of some sort.

Finn pulled me quickly down out of view - afraid we might be seen - and whispered a few words in my ear which filled me with new amazement. There seemed to be no end to the range of his strange abilities.

'I want to get a better view of one of them,' he said. 'I think I know that chap from somewhere … seen him around. If I can tap into his subconscious I might learn something.'

'You mean … you might be able to read his thoughts?' The idea was electrifying and I stared at him in disbelief.

'Something like that. I want to find out what this is all about.'

Stretching up to the window with due care, he focused his attention on the face of the man who had aroused his interest. And he stayed in that position for what I estimated to be a few short moments. It was obviously just enough time to carry out what he had in mind. Then he gestured to me to accompany him to the shelter of some fishing boats drawn up nearby, out of sight and hearing.

Even then he spoke in a low voice, shielding his face with one hand. 'It's as I suspected … a trick to get me here. They knew I wouldn't come willingly, so they watched for one of you to wander off a decent way from the cabin. Kyle was easy prey, as he's often about on his own.'

'But why would they want either of you?' I asked in surprise. 'And what use could Kyle be to them? He knows nothing of what goes on around here.'

'He was just a decoy. It's *me* they want. They know I'm gifted with second sight; that I can foretell certain things - like the weather - and would prove invaluable in leading them to those places to fish which others would not know. I could put a steady amount of money in their pockets that they could count on. They're questioning Kyle, hoping he'll lead them to me. They know I'll come looking for him eventually.'

Of course it all made sense then. I thought of this strange invulnerability Finn had, and his way of predicting things well in advance owing to the uniqueness of his senses; the reason his talents were so much sought after.

'But how can we rescue Kyle? I exclaimed, coming back to the question in hand. 'There's no way – not with three of them holding him.'

'Ah, but there's a few things they *don't* know about me, which you now *do*,' Finn replied, giving me one of his lop-sided grins, '...things which they would never dream of.'

'Oh,' I felt the colour rush to my face. 'You mean you can change yourself … your form … into another shape?'

Finn nodded. 'I think I'll be able to sort them out.'

'What will you change into?' I asked breath-lessly.

'Wait and see'.

I didn't have to wait long. It only took a few moments and, before my eyes, all that clothed Finn disappeared. His skin became furry, thick and grizzled; his body filled out growing broad and strong; and he grew four feet with large paws; his face became narrow and pointed with a broad snout. As he looked at me I saw that his eyes were amber coloured; sharp teeth showed beneath curling lips. And he boasted a long bushy tail.

'A *wolf*,' I breathed. And I would have been terrified had I not known it was Finn standing there. As it was, I think I was more fascinated than frightened. Of course there was no way we could warn Kyle of what was about to happen, and I suddenly became very worried on his behalf although I knew that no harm would befall him.

I watched from the window as the creature ambled over to the shed and pushed open the door. The men jumped to their feet with howls and cries of alarm, shouting and cursing loudly.

'What the hell … It's a wolf!'

'No wolves around here! Where did it come from?'

'Grab your rifle, Jake … Behind that pile o' wood.'

Goodness, I'd forgotten that one of them might have a firearm. Had Finn thought of that? He could be killed; a shapeshifter was just as vulnerable as we all were.

Finn obviously thought of it — just in time. Before the man could aim, he leapt out of the door. Then he hid behind the boats as before.

'Can't change to anything too outrageous, otherwise it will be in all the papers,' he muttered. 'Better to keep it within limits of understanding.'

I noticed that the man with the gun had appeared warily at the door, looking from left to right. It gave Finn just enough time to change into something else.

This time it was a large rat, and I wondered at this; anxious about how it would work. But I needn't have worried. It was a very large rat – a little larger than the imagination was prepared for.

It ran in through the door once again, but this time between the legs of the man who was still standing at the door. He almost dropped his rifle in surprise.

'What the devil …' he began. And he swung round to face the others in the room. Their faces were a picture. But I noticed that Kyle didn't seem that surprised. Obviously he had begun to put two and two together to some degree.

'What's going on around here?' roared another of the men.

The one with the gun pointed it at the rat, but it was much too quick and clever, diving and twisting this way and that. It isn't easy to kill a rat, I thought; even one of that size. It was almost as if it were playing a game with them. One of them dared to face it with a piece of wood ready to crush it, but it leapt straight at him and the man screamed dodging to one side at the last minute.

I watched unable to take my eyes from the scene as the creature looped its long tail round the leg of a chair sending it crashing down, and its occupant with it.

'Get the boy and let's go!' barked one of the men. They turned to grab him, but Kyle had wisely seized his chance amidst all the confusion and slid out unnoticed.

'Never mind him,' the man shouted. 'The wolf will probably get him … don't forget it's out there somewhere … have to report it.'

The three of them hurried from the shed, the foremost still nervously clutching his rifle; their voices eventually becoming fainter as they moved away.

Once Finn had joined us in his recognizable form, Kyle was full of praise.

'You were a fine rat!' he exclaimed. 'But I found the wolf a bit of a scare.'

Finn gave his lop-sided grin. 'Sorry about that – but there was no way we could warn you. The folk round here call me Marsh-rat, and that's what gave me the idea. Of course I had to be larger than large to make more of a stir.'

Kyle nodded, and then remembered something more. 'They were talking amongst themselves and said some boatmen promised them a good reward if they could find a way to lure you to them. It seems you might have made them a tidy profit.'

'That's the trouble with such men,' Finn replied. 'They see money in everything.'

5

While we had been away Finn's grandmother had been busy gathering crabs, eels, and small fruits and herbs for our supper. It was quite amazing how she could still do this at her great age. But I had to remind myself that she knew many things others could not begin to comprehend, and that explained a lot. She had already decided on some work for us later in the week.

We were to take Finn's dinghy and go fishing close to the shore to catch anything suitable that came along. The boat was an old one which had belonged to his grandfather, with a stubby mast, a set of oars, and a sail he had made himself. It was at once property and a source of food; the one thing of value he owned in the world.

It was decided some mackerel would make a change and we just had to wait for the right tide. Finn took a carp rod which he always used to good effect, and we set off on another adventure.

Of course I asked about the Sea Witch and if we would be at risk, but understood that as long as we stayed in the boat we were quite safe. In any case should there be any unforeseen occurrences we had the best bodyguard possible. And to this I had to agree.

So we set off in good spirits. First of all Finn rowed a bit until we reached deeper water, when we hoisted the sail. We didn't intend going far, but soon the wind caught us and the sail flapped and suddenly billowed full out. Then Finn had to tack back and fore in order to keep the wind at the right angle. We had forgotten all about the mackerel and needn't have come out so far.

Finn told us stories about places that lay under the ocean, and warned that the deeper one went, the colder and darker and more dangerous it became; for that was the kingdom of creatures like sharks, squid and sea snakes. And he told of somewhere far away called Wild Marsh where the reeds grew as high as trees. Any who set foot there would sink down to meet the Marsh King, he who ruled the quick-sands.

He pointed out some landmarks, especially Crag's Head, a cliff on the horizon which appeared to rise like an island from the sea. Once, he said, a monastery stood there which hundreds of years ago disappeared under the waves, and at certain times one could still hear its bell ringing. There was a causeway then which linked that part to the shore. But with the sinking of the land and the resultant marshes it gradually disappeared.

He told us how he became a sea bird and flew across the water to land on the mast of a passing ship. From there he dropped down to view what was now legend beneath the waves.

'What could you see?' Kyle asked, his eyes shining.

'As I hovered where the shafts of sunlight fell through the water I could clearly make out the ruins of the monastery, part of its walls still standing, and the remains of a stone roadway which must have led to it … and then I heard the bell ringing …'

'… *Under* the sea?' I breathed.

'*Under* the sea,' Finn repeated. 'It came to me

quite distinctly in a slow soft tone although it was so far below.'

'How ghostly,' Kyle replied in an awed voice.

'Ghostly it certainly was …' Finn's voice trailed off, as though he were thinking of something quite different. And then he said, 'The Sea Witch is of course related to the tides, the wind and weather.'

At this point he gave a shout and asked us to lend him a hand with the sail as quickly as possible. It was quite uncanny, since things began to change drastically from that moment. Hard fluky gusts struck from all directions, and the skies darkened, as if a silent curse had been uttered. The breeze began to bluster and the waves became choppy. The wind pushed us along at such speed we seemed to fly above the waves and very soon they increased in size, heaving us up and down so that our boat shuddered with the impact.

'How did you know this was coming?' I shouted above the howling wind.

'Saw a cloud I didn't like the look of,' Finn replied, shaking his head. 'The Sea Witch is up to something. Reckon I'll turn back.'

It was difficult to turn the boat in such a squall, but we managed it whilst the thunder growled around us and the rain threatened to wash us away.

And then we saw it … a fishing boat not far off. It throttled up its engine and began to head in our direction. As it drew closer we could make out one or two of its crew waving and shouting to us, and I recognized them as the same men we had encountered when Kyle was kidnapped. It was obvious their interest in us was far from friendly, and there was no way we could outrun them in our small boat.

I took a deep breath and turned to Finn to discover his reaction. Never in my wildest dreams could I have imagined what he did next.

Reaching into his pocket he took out his reed pipe and began to play. He did this with as much unconcern as if he were sitting outside his grandmother's cabin rather than the middle of the ocean on a rough sea facing hostile enemies. But then things happened in quick succession.

The storm blew itself out almost immediately and at the same time we discovered Finn was no longer with us. For an awful moment we thought he had decided to dive overboard. But a scene was unfolding before our eyes which was almost unbelievable. Although the sea had calmed, suddenly a wave of gigantic proportions began to heave and swell between us and the oncoming vessel. As we watched, a massive creature burst from the water narrowly missing and almost capsizing it.

'A whale,' Kyle gasped darting a quick glance at me. But I was bereft of words. If I had to describe it I would say it was like a bus rushing past, with an enormous swishing tail fin. We had never ever seen a whale before, so it was an amazing sight for us.

It soared through the water plunging towards us, blocking out the light.

The sight was terrifying enough, but to those on the fishing boat it must have been more so, since they were so much closer. It was twice the size of their boat and looked as though a building was about to fall on them or an avalanche engulf them. We thought it would drag their boat underwater but somehow it just missed it. The ripple of its powerful fin rocked them from side to side and they hung on for dear life. In fact our own little craft tossed about so much we wondered if we would be tipped overboard.

As we watched in wonder the whale repeated this performance once more, shooting up through the waves and then crashing down.

My mouth was dry. 'It's *huge!*' There were no words I could think of to describe it.

The crew of the fishing boat were obviously so afraid their boat would sink that they threw all of their day's catch overboard in an attempt to distract the monster and give them enough time to get away.

The fishermen were so awestruck that I reckoned it must have been the biggest fright they had had in their lives. It was unimaginable to think of a whale in these waters, let alone a giant one. I tried to imagine how they would try to explain this to anyone, especially after their dealings with us earlier.

We were by this time more excited than afraid and quite disappointed when the performance finally ended. The whale just disappeared beneath the waves as suddenly as it had come.

As for Finn, he could change in mood as the weather, and we were becoming used to his strange behaviour and habit of shapeshifting whenever the occasion warranted. So we were not greatly surprised to discover he had not deserted us, but was sitting in the exact position he had adopted sometime before.

But we could not imagine how exactly he could have masterminded such an amazing performance.

'We won't have much more trouble with *them*,' he announced with satisfaction as we put about, and made for shore.

We left behind a thoroughly drenched and shaken crew on the fishing boat, and guessed they would have an almost impossible task explaining the adventure that had befallen them on their way back from their fishing trip. Who would believe them?

'This will make big news all around the coast,' Kyle observed, to which I replied that they might decide not to say anything at all, for fear of being laughed at. Everyone would think they were joking.

Finn gave his lop-sided grin. 'At least you couldn't complain that your day was uneventful. But we'd better not forget the mackerel we were supposed to catch for our supper, otherwise *our* lives will not be worth living.'

We did in fact manage to bring several of these back once we within reach of the shore, and Finn's grandmother cooked the fish in oatmeal so they were not too oily. And they tasted very good.

6

Living on the marsh as we did most of the time and only occasionally venturing home, we came to familiarise ourselves with the elements. One of these was the sounds we heard. Often the wind had a different voice. We became used to its lonely and desolate cry, and somehow we knew it was also a part of the sea. When it lapsed to take a breath all became eerily quiet except for the passing sea birds calling in their haunting and mournful way.

As we journeyed further afield, we devised a way of leaving messages for each-other by tying knots in the cord grass or plaiting two or more together as tribal people used to do, to indicate in which direction we were and how far away.

I could quite understand how it took only special people to live as Finn and his grandmother did. During the time we were with them, the creeping atmosphere of the marsh with its seemingly endless space and loneliness attached itself to us, becoming part of us.

Our greatest memory of this was when we actually met the Sea Witch, or what we believed to be her. It was morning time, and we were returning from a trip in search of some thorn apple seeds for Finn's grandmother.

As we turned to face the shore, Kyle suddenly cried 'Look!' and pointed.

We saw a wall of white mist as high as a cliff looming ahead. It floated towards us, changing shape as it did so, at one point seeming like the ghostly sails of ships. Sea fog it was, ghostly, white, curling itself round us with long tentacles like some wild thing; writhing around our bodies in long trails and ropes, imprisoning us, since we could not see or think which way to move. It seemed that the very air was charged with suspense. It brought its own chill, a cold that seeped into us, like a paralysis, rendering us immobile.

We tried to cry out, but our words were swallowed by the dense blanketing cloud.

'I can't move,' Kyle exclaimed. 'I can't walk.'

'Close your eyes,' Finn told him. 'It will soon pass. Don't let it get to you.'

Easier said than done, I thought. But we did as he said, although the wind suddenly got up and began to howl around us with such a loud voice that the sound penetrated our senses. It stung our faces and hit out at us with spiteful gusts that tugged at our hair and brought tears to our eyes.

And then we saw her ... the Sea Witch.

Her face changed in shape and colour as she moved, and she appeared blue, then grey, then green, as she wound in and out from the curling mist, her waving hair caught by the wind making it flow and ripple in long strands. And all the while her white arms were reaching out with grasping fingers to draw us towards her.

It was no good me trying to convince Kyle that all was an illusion. He wouldn't believe me. And the long rolling waves of mist covered us so effectively that we were almost invisible to each-other.

'It's a trick,' I whispered. 'There's no-one there.'

But then as if to contradict me, most eerily of all, the Sea Witch's voice came to me quite clearly in the cold stillness. I thought afterwards that I might have dreamt it; that it was just the wind that had dropped to a whisper, the sound of water dripping or a muted bird song. But Kyle heard it also, so I knew it must be true.

Dark and cool with my arms so white,
Swim with me - come to the edge of night;
The edge that cuts like the sweep of a wand,
Opening doors to the space beyond;
Down through the gate where the whirlpools hide,
Through darkest depths past wind and tide;
Slide through the surf, slip through the swell,
Hear the sound of a lost church bell;
Leave the marshes and follow the waves
Down fathoms down to the kind sea caves;
There's none that venture will be so rich
As those that embrace the wild Sea Witch:
O strange earth children with strange drawn breath,
Watch where you walk – for the marsh brings death;
But my path leads to the treasures that are,
To the golden sands that await you afar;
Tread where I lead - let us join and bond,
Let us cross the edge to the space beyond.

But after she had spoken and we had remained in the same spot, she changed her tune. We saw the wraiths she brought up in an attempt to move and separate us: those forms of lost drowned sailors and travellers – ghosts from the deep. They were spectral figures, part of the mist that drove before the wakening wind.

I hid my face in my hands, and Kyle did the same. Only Finn remained calm. 'They are not real, though they appear so. Trust me.'

Afterwards the fog and mist lifted as suddenly as it came. Our breath seemed to hang on the air. We looked at each-other and laughed, for we were wet from head to toe, our hair sparkling like the dew on spiders' webs.

The experience was unnerving but dramatic. We felt sure it was somehow a warning to us. Afterwards we asked questions, and I remembered the Sea Witch's words about the sound of the church bell ringing under the sea. It did seem to fit somehow, although I couldn't guess what lay behind it.

However that was far from the end of it. The next day Finn told us of a dream he had during the night when the Sea Witch came to him as he lay half asleep. In the morning he found he could remember most of what was said, word for word.

'She accused me of using Earth magic; and I said that I used it only when I needed to. She then accused me of playing games, of calling up storms and changing the weather without her knowledge. She told how it was *her* breath that drew the tides and moved the winds with the moon's pull; that it was *she* who first made life; who sometimes took the land and sometimes gave it back. All things began and ended with her.

'I agreed with her, but said that most of earth's species now lived on the land. And at this she grew angry, saying that there were species unknown to me who dwelt in her kingdom.

'Again I agreed with her. But I told her that on land there's been a kind of race between plants and insects, and this has helped an amazing array of species. Land, I told her, is more productive than the cold, dark depths of the sea.

'She warned that the sea level is rising, and those who lived on land should take care.'

'What did you reply to that?' I asked, once Finn had paused to think of what came next.

'I advised that *she* should also take care since the world was warming and many of her creatures could not cope.'

'Do you remember her response?' I asked, thinking Finn might have forgotten.

'She was angry … said it was thanks to me and my kind. "For you pollute my kingdom,"' she said.

'I bowed my head at her words and could only respond weakly that we were trying to do something about it.'

He stopped here and gave us a wry look.

'What then?' I prompted.

'Oh, she just hissed at me, saying it was too little too late. And of course I had to once more agree with her.'

To have confided so much was a rare occurrence for him, and maybe he felt he had said too much. We were left to try and make of it what we could.

………

On several occasions after that I caught myself waiting and watching for those magical moments when, staring out to sea, the mist rolled out across the water so that sky, sea and land met and became one. On those occasions I pretended I could walk all the way across the water from one side to the other

With so much to think about, I found that Finn was beginning to stir strange and wonderful new concepts and ideas within me, amply repaying the care I lavished on our relationship.

One thing Kyle found amusing was the name the Sea Witch bestowed on us mortals, naming us 'earthworms'. We thought it a good enough description as things stood.

7

We had another unexpected adventure a few days later.

Kyle and I had just returned from an early evening trek after a rabbit we had seen and, arriving at the cabin, found Finn treating an injured crow.

'I get the feeling someone threw a stone purposely to do some damage,' he said, shaking his head.

'A farmer trying to scare it away from his fields,' Kyle suggested. 'That seems likely.'

'Maybe,' Finn replied, but he didn't look convinced.

We watched as he deftly examined it, muttering half to himself and half to the bird. We knew he had certain healing abilities as far as animals and birds were concerned.

'Strange that it's on its own and came this far out,' I said. 'Could be that it lost its way.'

'Not a chance,' Finn replied. 'Crows are clever birds; people are only now just beginning to learn *how* clever. It probably spied some carrion hereabouts.'

He fetched rainwater from the barrel outside the cabin and gave the bird some bread; he then made a kind of perch close by where it sat surveying us with its bright beady eyes.

We fully expected that was the last we'd see of it, but to our surprise it stayed around the cabin for a few days. We fed it on scraps, so obviously it knew we would look after it. Then it disappeared for another few days, and we really thought we'd lost it this time. But back it came as before, now carrying something tied to its leg.

It was a message scrawled on a scrap of paper inserted in a tiny tube. Obviously the bird had been used to carrying messages in the past and was clever enough to find its way back to us.

Finn read the message which was very short and to the point: *Help … Prisoner … old mill Steeply.*

It was all most mysterious and exciting. Of course we made wild assumptions as to *who* could be the prisoner - and *why*. Steeply was a small village some miles inland, Finn said; but he had never heard of anyone mention an old mill thereabouts.

Our only course of action was to set off as soon as we were able, and this we decided to do, starting out early the next morning, taking with us a few things we might need such as a rope, a supply of water and some food in our back-packs.

The crow flew on ahead of us, but not far enough for us to lose sight of him; now and again proving his trust by perching on Finn's shoulder.

Our journey passed pleasantly enough, and we pointed out to each-other the various forms of wildlife we encountered along the way. But eventually we left the marsh behind with its winding ways and circling sea-birds, and came to a sunken road where we had to cross some fields and climb a gate. Then the ground started to climb gradually, and we found ourselves on the outskirts of the village. Steeply was a good name for it, we decided.

We stopped close to an old inn and refreshed ourselves with a few sandwiches, then looked around for someone to ask for directions to the mill, hoping to pick up any local news which might give a clue as to what was happening in the area.

Luckily we chanced upon a local man on his way out from the inn, and introduced ourselves. Having explained that we were interested in bird watching and were looking for an owl's nest, we asked if we were taking the right path to the mill.

At mention of this he shook his head vehemently, and warned us away, muttering under his breath. It was with some persuasion that we managed to get the story from him surrounding the local news.

Apparently a small group of travellers had entered the village distributing their wares, which consisted of dried herbs they had grown themselves. Good for healing a variety of known health complaints, they said. But several of the locals had ended up with bad bouts of fever, and the doctor told them it was the result of the herbs which were dangerous. They managed to catch one of them, a girl, and several of the locals took the law into their own hands, imprisoning her in the old mill. She'd been there for a few days in the ruin at the back of the village while they decided what to do with her.

'That's a right devilment,' the man pointed out. 'Selling herbs that ain't right is agin' the law; it's a felony. She be a witch I'll be bound.'

So at least we knew what we were up against. But it left us in the unenviable position of not quite knowing what to do about it.

'The girl might not have realized the dangers,' I pointed out. 'Surely one should give her the benefit of the doubt. To accuse and imprison her in such a way seems very wrong.'

We looked at Finn for advice but he almost ignored us, shaking his head and cursing under his breath. But he waved us onwards all the same.

I glanced at Kyle and he shrugged, so with one mind we followed without question and waited to see what awaited us.

8

All this time the crow had flown ahead of us, as if to reassure us that we were on the right track. Our path led us towards land which fell away sharply in one place and where at the topmost ridge of the hill there stood the black ruin of a windmill. It had no sails and from where we stood we could clearly see the sky showing through the roof.

The sun had suddenly disappeared and heavy clouds were blowing up from the seaward side making the old ruin even more gaunt and lonely.

There didn't seem to be anyone nearby, but we were on one of the most exposed places for miles around so stood a very good chance of being seen. As we warily approached the shelter of the building I wondered if the girl prisoner might be able to see us from her vantage point up above.

'There must be a doorway somewhere,' Kyle exclaimed, echoing my thoughts. And I turned to Finn to see what response he might give.

'This way,' he motioned, turning towards some crumbling stone steps. And I saw an entrance which led up to a gaping hole in the wall above his head.

I realized that this would have been the first floor, in which case there must be another way to reach the one further up. Rooting around, we soon discovered a ladder half hidden by timbers which we propped against the next level and quickly scrambled up. It would have proved impossible for anyone to come or go without using this, on account of the height.

The prisoner was crouched in a corner - just a slip of a girl - white faced, with wide frightened eyes. Beside her was a small tray on which lay the remains of a half-eaten crust of bread and a jug of water.

We hastened to explain that we had come in response to her message for help which was sent by her bird messenger.

At this her face brightened. She nodded and pointed to the crow, which as we spoke flew in through the open roof to perch on her shoulder.

Then she related a little of her story. Her name was Carys, and she told how she was with a group of travellers that wandered from place to place selling small items like wooden bowls, pieces of jewellery and painted stoneware. She also sold some of her herbs which she insisted were quite safe – unless anyone proved allergic to them – which is what she thought must have happened since several people had become ill. Someone had accused her of being a witch and saying that her herbs were poisonous. From then on, more and more people came forward to accuse her.

The crow was a pet of hers, one she had rescued from a tree fall when young. She called it Jac, because she thought at first it was a jackdaw. It had grown used to carrying messages for her, and on this occasion might have saved her life since she was uncertain what fate awaited her.

It was obvious to us that the girl was genuinely distressed by what had happened and we decided to do all we could to help her. Having used the ladder once again—this time to make our exit—we grouped together outside to determine our next move. Being undecided at this point we carried on down the hill, but were surprised to see crowds of people gathered there. In fact it looked as though half the village had turned up.

They were led by the very same man who had warned us away from the mill when we asked for directions. He was angrily waving his stick, and shouting abuse. There was no way we could make our escape.

And then it seemed that a miracle happened. From somewhere above our heads we heard the harsh rasping cry of a crow. Looking skywards we realized it was a signal to others; a huge flock began to gather, cawing and screeching, circling and soaring, dropping down lower and lower towards the crowd below. As we watched in wonder we saw that they drew more and more to their numbers. Almost in minutes as everyone watched with bated breath, the sky was filled with a gigantic dark blanket.

Then they began their attack. They landed where they could, on nearby trees and on people's heads, striking out with their sharp beaks. With black flashing wings, deadly black eyes and black beaks, they swarmed on all those they recognized as enemies.

Their screeches filled the air. We watched with fascinated horror at the brutal assault as the birds clawed and pecked mercilessly. It became a kind of war zone. There were even several instances where their talons got stuck in people's hair.

The crowds that had gathered were soon dispatched screaming and shrieking in terror and pain.

'It was Jac that alerted them,' Carys explained once we were alone together. 'Crows are such intelligent creatures, almost as clever as humans.'

Finn gave one of his lop-sided grins at that, and patted her on the back. 'You're right,' he said. 'But people don't realize how formidable they can be once they become angry. They usually only protect their own – and your pet obviously considers you as one of its kind. But since we were with you, we were also included and kept safe. No creature forgets a kindness, but few will repay it in kind.'

I felt the incident was something we would remember for some time to come. Meanwhile we wondered what would become of Carys, for it would be foolish and dangerous for her to be seen anywhere near the village.

'Come with us,' Finn advised. 'No-one will approach or harm us; they're all much too scared.' He grinned. 'They're probably even more convinced that you're a witch now - when even the birds of the air come to your aid.'

'And crows have a bad reputation for evil doings,' Kyle responded. 'So that will add to all their superstitions.'

Carys appeared comforted by this; although she insisted that she was well able to care for herself. 'I will go back with you until we reach the edge of the marsh,' she said, 'and then I will just melt into the green.'

Before we left the outskirts of Steeply, she told us a little about the place and why she felt interested enough to travel there. We were surprised to learn how much she knew about the land. 'The old mill was flooded years ago, and all around here was once covered by water,' she said. 'But gradually the sea receded and the local people reclaimed and worked the land so it became arable and farms grew up all around.'

We looked at each-other and I knew the three of us were thinking about the Sea Witch and how the ground we stood upon once belonged to her.

Before we parted Finn warned Carys to be more careful how she used her herbs in future, and she promised to do this.

We were quite sorry to lose our new friend, but very glad that our adventure had turned out as well as it did in the end.

9

One day we had a visitor; someone who had travelled quite a distance to see us. This was quite a rare occurrence in our part of the world, where few strangers ventured. But although the person was a stranger to Finn, Kyle and me, he was not considered so by Finn's grandmother. It turned out that the old man in question was an acquaintance of hers going back many years.

He was once a fisherman who had visited many places and had quite a few stories to tell, some of a rather strange nature. And since stories were one thing that Finn's grandmother couldn't get enough of; these were something we were all eager to share.

It was during the evening time that we usually got together building our fire on sticks above the ground, enjoying the sound of the flames as they hissed and spat and the sucking gurgle of the marsh mingled with the lap of distant waves.

Cedric, as he was named, was tall and thin of stature and despite his years remained fit and active. The silver white hair drawn back from his brow gave his gaunt features a certain austere appearance; but his brown eyes creased into smiles every so often, by which I detected a certain sense of humour.

There was one of his tales in particular that caught and held my imagination. It was a telling that could be described as 'a tale within a tale'. As Cedric explained it was not necessarily believable, but there was sure to be a moral in it somewhere if we looked deeply enough.

'Some years ago,' he said, 'a certain tradesman took a journey across some marshland - rather like *this* marsh - except that it lay on the banks of a river. Feeling rather tired, he sat down and took some bread and a few plums out of a bag he had with him. As he ate the plums he threw the stones into one of the pools that lay around him.

Having finished his meal, he decided to continue on his journey as before. But just as he was about to do so, something black and quite hideous leapt out from the water and landed at his feet. It was a creature with a frog's head and the body and legs of a grotesque goblin.

The little creature jumped up and down in an obvious rage, shrieking in an angry voice. It took the astounded and frightened traveller some time to realize what had happened, but luckily due to his practice of reading minds he was at last given to understand that one of his plum stones thrown so thoughtlessly had mortally wounded one of the frog-goblin's kinsfolk.

The frightened and dismayed man begged for forgiveness, but the creature made a bargain with him. He would give him one year in which to return to his family and settle his affairs, but after that time he must return to the same spot on the marsh to meet the punishment that would be meted out to him. He warned that should he fail to arrive he was sure to be found wherever he was. There was no hope of escape.

So exactly a year later the poor man arrived at the same place and waited to hear the verdict. He did not have to wait long. The loathsome frog-goblin appeared suddenly from a pool close by, and cried out "Are you ready to face your punishment?"'

The man immediately begged for mercy as before, but added that upon making enquiries he had learnt that frog-goblins were very fond of travellers' tales; and he thought he had a good one which he hoped might help to soften his sentence.

The frog-goblin who loved to listen to a good story, agreed to this, and said that if the story pleased him he would be tempted to forgive the crime which after all had been committed in all innocence.'

At this point Cedric paused in his telling, and faced us with an inscrutable smile. We waited impatiently, but there was a long silence. And at last I asked if he had maybe forgotten the second part of the story.

'Not at all,' he replied. 'But it will do for another sitting … maybe tomorrow.' And we had to be content with that.

10

When we returned the following evening, we were all eager to hear the rest of what Cedric had to say. And he continued with the tradesman's tale, as told to the frog goblin:

'One day, a fishing boat and its crew are overtaken far out at sea by a terrific storm. They struggle to keep afloat but eventually all are lost except one young lad who manages to hold on to some of the rigging. Eventually he is washed ashore on a strange island where he tries to take stock of his bearings. He barely has enough time to look round when he hears thunder; the earth shakes and releases a giant serpent, the like of which he has never before imagined.

He wonders if he is still merely half conscious, tossed about by the waves and still clinging to the piece of wreck. The fact that the monster *speaks* to him seems even more unbelievable.

'"Who brings you here?" it asks. And the boy cannot answer for he forgets how he came there. But the creature asks again, "Answer or you die."

In desperation the boy remembers something he carries with him … a good luck charm he is never without that has survived the shipwreck. Lifting it carefully from his pocket, he offers it to the serpent. It is a pearl of great size and beauty which he discovered one day when diving below the sea.

'"Will you accept this treasure?" he asks the serpent, all the while trembling from head to toe.

The serpent's eyes grow wide and he slides over to snatch it greedily. But at that moment a great wave rises up behind them and a whale of awesome and monstrous size appears. With one snap of its huge jaws it swallows the pearl! The serpent, cheated of its prize, turns upon the boy in rage. The terrified boy without stopping to think leaps quickly into the sea in the wake of the whale and is soon sucked below the waves.

The pearl is gone - and he will be next. That much is sure. But he soon discovers that he can breathe underwater as effortlessly as the many fish he sees around him – another reason to believe he must be dreaming.

It is then that he hears the whale's song, booming and echoing under the water, and words seem to form themselves in his head: *This way … swim this way … where the seals play.*

He swims further on towards the coast, and there he finds to his amazement a group of seals nosing the lost pearl to one another. Maybe the whale spat it out in a fit of coughing, as he'd seen whales do sometimes.

If you want it – come and get it, they seem to say, taunting him. They disappear into a nearby cave while the boy follows; feeling his way like a blind thing for the cave is deep and dark as a tomb. But as his eyes quickly grow accustomed to the dark, he becomes aware of a danger which threatens hiding in the shallows.

A tiger shark, it is, watching the seals; waiting to make a kill. The boy warns them by whistling to them.

Once aware of the danger the seals make their escape with the boy grabbing desperately at one of their tails and hanging on as they strike for the surface. The pearl is forgotten – but not by the seals as they turn frantically to make for deeper water. One of them tosses it to him as a mark of thanks and farewell. Then they leave quickly and the boy realizes he's within sight of the shore.

Just as he breathes a sigh of relief, something very large thrusts itself against him. It must be the shark which has followed him. But no … it's a turtle … a very large one that is swimming near the surface. Its huge shell has bumped into him almost as if it intends to give him a lift. Hanging on, he uses it as a vehicle to propel him through the water. In this manner he manages to reach the beach.

So things have turned in a circle, and he finds himself back where he started on the island – wondering whether he dreamt it all.

This was the story as told to the frog-goblin by the traveller on the marsh. And having completed his tale, he waits to hear how it has been received. The frog-goblin is well pleased, having found the story most entertaining and grants the teller's request for a pardon, leaving him with a warning of being more careful in future how he disposes of his plum stones!'

We all laughed at this, but Finn's grandmother shook her head and made a point of saying 'Sum-mat to listen to, I grant, but just another of them old fireside travellers' tales.'

'Which is what it was supposed to be, Grandma,' Cedric remarked with a grin.

'And the moral of the story,' Kyle piped up, 'is not to go throwing plum stones around in marshes.'

I think we all felt there was not much more we could add to that.

11

While some people might be gifted with a sixth sense or premonition about something that is about to happen, or has happened, Finn could go a step further. He could be drawn to the exact spot where an unknown incident was taking place.

'It's not anything you can change, even if you want to,' he explained; and that was one of the reasons he was content to live the life he did, otherwise he would be assailed with all the many problems society demanded.

An example of this was when we were fishing along the shore one afternoon and he suddenly stopped halfway through a sentence. With a startled exclamation, he turned and looked out across the sea.

'Quick! Turn around! Make for Crags Head!'

We knew better than to ask questions. Brought up alongside the fisher folk, we were used to all kinds of life and death situations at sea and our scuba gear was something we always kept handy when sailing.

Finn knew exactly where we were going, and explained as we went. A sudden photographic image had exploded in his brain and unfolded before him. Someone was trapped in the old wreck which lay below Crags Head. Divers often went there to explore the ship unaware of the dangers that threatened.

The person was alone, trapped or injured in some way. So desperate was his plight that he had scrawled a last message in the sand beside him, presumably for one of his family.

We soon located his small skiff, anchored with the main line still attached. It was simply a matter of making a few quick calculations and then positioning our own boat which Kyle would stay with, while Finn and I made the dive.

The area was well known to the coast guards who always recommended that they were informed about a proposed dive, but many disregarded this advice and went it alone.

Finn knew the area well. As soon as the sinister outline of the wreck loomed into view, he motioned for me to keep back while he went in front to make sure the way was clear.

Suddenly a sound startled me, a muffled long rumbling vibration that reached me through the water as if from a great distance.

'Whatever's that?' I asked.

'It's the voice of a whale,' Finn replied. 'It's the way they speak to contact one another from great distances under the ocean. Some say they are singing, but their mouths are tightly closed when they make those sounds. So they *hum* – not sing.'

And I remembered that the old fisherman we met had spoken of the whale in his folk tales when he came to visit.

My attention was next drawn to the many shoals of fish which drifted around me and I watched fascinated as a large stingray emerged from a cavernous hole in the hull looking for prey. How it got there I had no idea. They weren't usually seen in the waters we travelled, and I wondered if the Sea Witch had anything to do with it.

Just then Finn beckoned to me, but as I approached, he suddenly changed his mind and urgently waved me back. I saw at once what the problem was.

An octopus of no mean size was blocking his entry to the submerged part of the vessel he wanted to access. It was obviously intending to protect its territory from invaders, and I wondered what Finn *would* or *could* do considering that time was of the essence.

My attention was distracted for a moment as I lurched to one side to avoid a stingray, and when I next focused on the scene the octopus was grappling with a large conger eel.

Watching in fascinated horror I was sure the octopus would win. It whipped its muscular tentacles round the body of the eel grasping it tightly with its eight arms. But the opposite happened. The eel bit into its opponent fiercely, and I recalled that it had two jaws with sharp teeth. The octopus struggled to free itself and, finding that was impossible, released an angry ink cloud. I was just in time to see that the eel had bitten off one of its arms. Not the greatest tragedy to an octopus since it would soon grow another but it made the short battle that bit more dramatic.

When the water cleared, the octopus had disappeared, and Finn was already swimming into the space where the injured diver lay.

As it happened the young man in question was not injured, only trapped beneath a large timber plank which had fallen across one leg; a common enough occurrence in old wrecks. But his air supply was almost at the point of running out. It was imperative that we got him up to the surface as quickly as possible.

With both of us supporting him on either side, we propelled him to the surface.

Kyle was waiting above in the boat, and as soon as we appeared he gave a relieved shout. 'I've got him!' he yelled. 'Haul him up!'

The young man's leg, although badly bruised, did not appear broken. By the time we had wrapped him in Finn's jacket, he was ready to relate some of the horror he had experienced upon finding himself alone with no help available.

'I can't believe you found me,' he exclaimed. 'I really thought my time was up.'

We explained that we just happened to be in the right spot and that he was very lucky we had discovered him. Having said this, we hardly needed to warn him of the dangers of wreck diving on his own and felt sure he would not be making the same mistake twice.

By the time we had got to harbour with his boat in tow he looked none the worse for his adventure. However we advised him to keep quiet about his escapade which he promised to do. We didn't want the coastguards asking any awkward questions.

12

Very early one morning we had an unnerving experience. There was a loud scratching, scraping, and a series of frenzied screeches coming from the roof of the cabin.

We rushed outside but first of all could see nothing in the early fog that had crept in from the sea. At last we were able to discern the outline of a bird that was frantically causing all the commotion.

'It's a crow – or one of that family,' Finn exclaimed, shading his eyes as he tried to get a better view. 'And it's trying to tell us something.'

A crow indeed it was and a very large and rather familiar one at that. We couldn't think for a moment where we had seen it before.

Then it came to us quite suddenly.

It was Jac, the crow that belonged to our friend Carys, the girl we had rescued from the old mill at Steeply. It had brought us a message from her then, and now seemed to be in great distress over something.

It obviously remembered Finn and flew down and settled on his shoulder. But then it rose in the air with loud cries, circling a little ahead of us.

'It wants us to follow it,' Kyle exclaimed.

'And wants us quickly, I should say,' I added. 'Carys must be in trouble somewhere.'

'Somewhere not far away,' Finn said, looking grim.

Without stopping to think further we hurriedly followed in the crow's direction. Along the shore a little further we came to a place where the marsh was particularly treacherous. The fog had lifted a little more now, and we were able to make out our poor friend Carys, with just her arms showing above her head, being slowly sucked down in the watery mire.

'Hold on! We're here!' I cried. But I wondered what we could do, since we needed a rope - which we hadn't got - and it looked as though it was already too late for that.

At that moment the crow suddenly gave a loud squawk, and looking round we found that Finn had disappeared.

Then I recalled that in moments of extreme stress he told me he had the power to shape-change. But into *what* had he changed?

We found this out very quickly. A huge snake of a size not seen anywhere in our waters, quickly wound its way towards the struggling girl.

I screamed out just in time, to warn her. 'Trust us, Carys! Just trust us!' And she became still, out of exhaustion more than anything.

It must have been a horrifying ordeal when the big snake wrapped her in its coils, although I guessed by the time this happened she had become almost unconscious with the cold and fear anyway.

Kyle and I watched in a mixture of profound awe and wonder as the huge creature twisted itself round the girl. We were afraid she would be crushed by its immense size but as it encircled her it made a large loop around her body lifting her slowly and carefully out from the grip of the treacherous mud. We heard the loud sucking noise as she appeared and saw the snake gradually draw her with it to firmer ground where she at lay in a sort of crumpled heap.

We rushed over to her and carried her between us to the cabin where we wrapped her in blankets. Grandma gave her hot drinks, and she eventually revived enough to tell us her story.

'I wanted to try and find you again, and I started out really early. I should have waited until the fog lifted, but I thought I could see a light out towards the shore … it must have been from your cabin. It drew me … but I lost the path … and then the tide started coming in. The ground suddenly got very swampy and I went in up to my waist. Luckily Jac was close by and he then flew off in what I hoped was an attempt to find you. I began to panic as I slowly began to sink. Then everything went dark and I think I must have passed out.'

Finn, Kyle and I just looked at each-other. We were thankful she couldn't remember anything more. We all praised Jac, who strutted about in such a cocky way that we were certain he knew what a hero he was.

That evening, to take her mind off things, Finn produced his reed pipe and explained how he made the sounds. Carys wanted to try, but the notes came out all wrong and made us laugh. So Finn played some of his own soulful tunes which calmed and helped us get in the mood for sleep.

Somehow we made room in the cabin, and Carys spent the night cuddled up to me. The next day we took her back over the marsh to a safe place where she could continue her travels. Like Finn she was a rather special individual who enjoyed her own company although she did at times join up with other travellers like herself. As she said, she was never really alone since she had Jac for a friend.

13

Since it is me, Morgan, who is relating this story, I feel that I should not leave out the stranger on four legs that one day paid us a visit. This was no other than *a cat* – who mysteriously appeared – sitting with perfect composure and a certain amount of cockiness at the stern of our boat, almost as if to say 'I have every right to be here.'

It was certainly a strange cat; all skin and bones and most unattractive, with a character to match. It was small in size, dull grey in colour, and still agile although walking with a slight limp.

Having made its entrance, it spent its time scrabbling about at the water's edge and pouncing upon things in pools catching small crabs or whatever came its way.

Nothing remarkable about that, one might say, but this cat had certain traits which singled it out from others we had come across.

For one thing it seemed quite oblivious to our presence most of the time, except on the odd occasion when it did notice us and showed an obvious fear and dislike of humans. But Finn, we knew, could create a certain aura irresistible to animals once he had formed some sort of contact.

'Did you know,' he said, 'that cat's eyes are windows to another world? He then went on to tell us that most animals didn't like being stared at, including the cat. But this was something he intended to do in this case.

'It's the only way I can connect with its previous lives – for this cat has lived before on several different occasions.'

This news took our breath away. Of course we'd heard that cats reputedly had nine lives due to their amazing ability to overcome danger, so we decided this was just Finn's way of explaining how he believed this particular cat had survived many such incidents. However we were curious to see what would happen.

Having seated himself in a prominent position, Finn emitted a whistling call—not unlike that of some bird—in order to gain the cat's attention.

It immediately froze in its tracks; then slowly approached while Kyle and I watched from some distance away.

Eventually it came quite close, and both the cat and Finn seemed to stare mesmerised at one another. It was as if Finn was prodding it with his thoughts, to make it understand that he was a friend. This lasted for some moments until at last they drew apart, and the cat went on its way.

Finn explained that the information he had gathered was primarily the creature's natural affinity with boats. Boats meant fishing and food one way or the other, although how it had discovered and boarded ours was a mystery.

'But it must be dreadful for it, just living off scraps, out in all weathers with no shelter,' Kyle exclaimed.

'It will always find somewhere – some hollow or hole in which it can survive. It lives by its wits,' Finn said. 'There's many a house cat that walks off into the wilderness and fends for itself as efficiently as its ancestors did thousands of years ago.'

And we looked upon the cat with different

eyes from that day on. It stayed around for some time, and we called it Misty on account of its dark grey colour which seemed to blend in very well with the marsh mist.

Although she wouldn't allow us to touch her or get close, Misty seemed eager to set off in our boat. She stood proudly at the bow looking out at sea, reminding us of one of the figure-heads used on sailing vessels to remind sailors that the ship was a living thing. In fact Kyle suggested that he should paint her new name on the side of the boat.

There was only one incident which might have ended badly which I recall. And that was when a sudden squall caught us not far from shore and Misty fell overboard.

There she was, struggling in deep, very cold salt water, striking out frantically with her four legs, yowling loudly, whilst her panic and the sea water were almost choking her.

Finn threw a net overboard and managed to haul her up, and I rubbed her dry with an old towel. We soon learnt that kindness was something unknown to her.

Once the wind had abated a bit, Misty was able to stand and walk unsteadily. And what a spectacle she was! Thin, gawky, with damp fur standing out in all directions.

With difficulty we managed to get her back to the cabin where Grandma fed her on scraps of cooked fish and some watered-down evaporated milk, something completely alien to her, yet which she appeared to enjoy immensely.

Finn continued to be quite concerned about the little creature. 'She regards everyone as a potential enemy to be treated with the utmost suspicion,' he explained.

Shortly after this incident we found that her attitude towards us had changed. A door had been left open in one corner of the cabin and Misty had crept inside. There she was, curled up seemingly quite at home. It must have been bliss to her, to find warmth and shelter - something she was so unused to.

After this she became more trusting and if one of us slowly stretched out a hand – making her aware of our intentions – she touched the hand with her nose. Then, if a tit-bit was offered, she fell upon it with relish. Friendship and fish went together she had obviously decided.

But it became apparent to us that Misty much preferred to be afloat than on land, and we thought it might be that she connected land with trouble of one sort or another.

This was borne out by an old fisherman - another acquaintance of Grandma's - who called to see us, and who at once recognized our cat friend.

The old fellow squinted, half closing his eyes, and pointed a finger. 'Why … how did that there varmint turn up 'ere?'

'We were wondering the same thing,' Kyle piped up, before I could answer.

Then I asked how he knew of her, and that we had named her Misty.

'Misty … that's what ye call the blighter? Always stows away on our boats after our catch. But blown if I knows 'ow she got all way out 'ere on t' marsh.'

'It's a mystery,' Finn nodded. 'But what do you know of her round your parts?'

'Why, 'tis said she's 'ad plenty mis'aps; used up all of 'er nine lives I'd say. 'tis a wonder she's still around.'

Kyle looked at me, and I looked at him.

'Can you tell us what you know …' I ventured.

And we sat around in the cabin eating some of Grandma's herb cakes while he told us what he could remember of Misty's past history.

…………

'She be a reg'lar seafaring cat. Creeps on board 'fore anyone be aware. She bin and fell overboard more 'n once. Ye'd think she'd ha' learnt 'er lesson. She be lucky we hauled 'er back – 'cos she be a reg'lar little varmint most times. She be not quite a black cat, d' ye see? Black be unlucky to sailors and such like.'

We told him that we'd heard that cats have nine lives, and he laughed.

'Ships cats need 'em,' he said. And he went on. 'She 've got salt on 'er tail, that un.'

'And salt on her whiskers,' Kyle added.

The old man nodded. 'Aye, she be a rare 'n that 'n.'

It appeared that Misty had survived against all odds. There was one instance where she had been attacked by a savage dog and was badly wounded. However she managed to crawl away and was found by one of the fishermen's wives who took pity on her and nursed her.

On another occasion she was targeted by children who took pleasure in cruel games, and she was almost stoned to death. No-one thought she would recover after that. But she did.

She had also survived the bitter cold and snow when the sheds used by the fishermen were closed for winter. At another time she got shut in, and went without food and water for weeks.

The list of her desperate experiences went on and on. We thanked our visitor for enlightening us on Misty's sad past, and then wondered what was to become of her.

She obviously enjoyed her time with us, especially when she sampled Grandma's cooked food – something she had never experienced before. But when the old fisherman began to make ready to sail with his much bigger and more enticing vessel, she quickly decided where her options lay. A boat was a boat after all, and something she had long associations with. Maybe she felt unable to live under a roof for any length of time.

The last we saw of her was sitting at the bow of the fishing boat looking out to sea like the figure-head she obviously intended to be

14

We loved and hated the sea both at the same time. We loved it when we heard it laughing and flinging its spray skywards, when it gurgled and dreamed among its many pools; we hated it when each day we saw it stealing more and more of the land. And we knew that the land and sea were fighting each-other and that the land was trying to claw back what it was losing, little by little.

Finn told us stories about the marsh to keep our imagination alive in case we should forget its history and magic. He told us about smugglers and ghost ships; of strange lights that appeared without warning at night; and creatures that were not of our world. It was quite extraordinary how things could change in an instant. You only had to close your eyes for a second or blink to find yourself in another dimension.

'Don't go wandering around outside at night,' Finn warned us. And only once had I ignored his advice. We were aware of unearthly things haunting and prowling the marshes – we'd heard the cries and the muffled footsteps; the weird knocking and rattling outside the door which we knew was not that of the wind. But on that one night I ignored the warnings.

I was woken by a sudden scratching outside the window. Just some small creature, I thought. Then I saw a white face peering in through the glass. Could it be a trick of the moonlight? I slipped quietly out of my narrow bed, grabbed a torch and began pulling on my boots, oblivious to Kyle who lay close by. I was almost at the door when a muffled voice reached me, hardly above a whisper.

'Wait … don't go … wait for me!' Kyle sat upright, waved frantically, and staggered to his feet. In another instant he had slipped on his boots and a mac, and followed me outside.

I was suddenly glad of his presence. It was cold, damp, and decidedly unfriendly out there. The sound of the wind along the shore wailed dismally like the voices of women and children, reminding me of those drowned souls Finn often talked about. I shone my torch ahead, but only intended going a little way just to set my mind at rest, looking to right and left, trudging along in silence. However, the track seemed to grow more unfamiliar with each step. Kyle noticed it too. He walked beside me with chattering teeth, not only from the cold I was sure.

I was beginning to wish we had never left the cabin yet I urged him on anyway. But we saw nothing and no-one, and after a few more moments I felt him tugging at my sleeve.

'Let's go back,' he muttered, his teeth still chattering. I agreed, since there seemed no point in continuing, and the warmth of our beds called. We turned round to face the way we had come.

But we'd left it too late.

Looking down I became suddenly aware of what appeared to be a mass of bright staring eyes peering up at me like drops of starlight spreading out on either side of my feet. As I moved, so they moved, keeping pace with me almost as they were lighting my way. Kyle was a little way behind. I could hear him panting to keep up. I tried not to look down and shone my torch before me. But the eyes drew ahead of me as if leading me on, and if I tried moving away to one side they hemmed me in, surrounding me. It was impossible to avoid looking at them.

I turned to Kyle. Could he see them too? But he appeared to be listening rather than looking, and I began to hear what *he* could hear: voices that gurgled and gulped like water bubbling up from some underground spring. I began to run, stumbling as I went, but the quicker I moved the less distance there was between me and the nightmare I tried to escape from.

Then all at once the eyes disappeared and I gasped in relief. But they were only replaced by something even more terrifying – long arms which stretched up towards me, at the ends of which were sinewy hands with claw-like fingers ready to grasp my legs as I struggled to keep a foothold on the swampy bog. A sudden image flashed before me of Carys, the girl Finn had rescued, being sucked into the black depths only a few days earlier.

The voices of whatever lay beneath me changed from gurgling sounds to a croaking and hissing, and a dozen hands dragged me backwards and down as I sank deeper into the mire.

I had dropped my torch. I groped around blindly as the creeping horror threatened to engulf me. Then a menacing growl rent the air. A dark shape leapt up in front of me. A pair of eyes, red and glowing stared down at me.

I screamed.

I heard Kyle shout.

The phantom before me appeared to be that of a large dog or wolf. And just as I thought my end was certain, I heard several high-pitched cries. The nightmare hands shrivelled in the burning light of the beast's eyes, and then all went dark.

Strong arms pulled me free, and I heard a loud 'glug' as my legs were released from the bog.

Kyle was lucky. He had just escaped the dangerous patch of swamp I had wandered into. But he'd seen it all: the hands that grew arms and the beast with its red burning eyes. He explained all that had happened during those moments when my senses had apparently left me.

We thought we had been on our own, but once again Finn had followed us rescuing us from yet another nightmare. We couldn't hide things from him. He knew everything.

If Kyle hadn't been there I would have thought that I imagined the whole thing. And there are those who insist that under such circumstances imagination often runs wild; that terrifying experiences have been recorded from folk out on the marshes at night. Such an environment can be full of unexplained mysteries: sinister moving shadows appearing among the tall grasses and reeds; strange noises erupting from mud pools; and the glowing eyes of creatures roaming through the darkness. And I wondered if it was a kind of lesson – a warning meted out to those who dared to go wandering about at night in eerie, ghostly places.

Dawn was already creeping across the marsh filling the dark hollows with light as we scrambled back into our narrow bunks.

15

I remember sitting beside one of the fires we often made outside the cabin on quiet evenings when we were watching the moon rise over the sea mist, listening to the laughing croak of the marsh frogs. It seemed that the space around us was spread out at the edge of the world, as if it were under some sort of spell which wouldn't end until it was unravelled.

Finn was playing on his pipe and the sound rode softly on the breeze making me feel particularly dreamy.

Then the talk of dragons came up, and as usual old Grandma muttered at the stories—as she often did—saying they were old tales from her great, great, great grandmother's time.

But Finn shrugged and shook his head. 'Who's to say how true or untrue they are. Any tale handed down must have a grain of truth in it somewhere. Or how else could it survive?'

I was only half listening. There was some magic about that night, and I stared into the glowing embers of the fire imagining them to be the eyes of a dragon. It was then that I became aware of *someone* or *something* that was there beside me.

My heart began to race. I heard a voice calling me—but I had no voice to answer. I followed, drawn against my will. The voice called again, so sweetly this time that I felt there was no harm in it. Then I looked before me and saw the grasses parting making a pathway for me to follow—yet there were no trace of footprints. All I could feel was the magic of it, and the sudden passing of a cold, cold wind.

It seemed that I crossed the marsh and stopped almost at the water's edge. And I knew I had been led there and had followed in the steps of the Sea Witch.

Finn was with her. Their voices were low, like the sound of waves lapping on the shore, and yet I could hear every word that was spoken.

'You want land – I will give you land – but what will you give *me* in return?'

'What do you want from me?'

'If I ask for nothing you will still continue in your old ways working at how to get the better of me. And so I ask one thing. Since from water you came at the beginning, so must you return. Those are my terms. Do we agree?'

I woke to find Kyle prodding me. He said I had been sitting like one in a trance, neither asleep nor fully awake.

I looked across at Finn and he also admitted to dreaming, but he said the Sea Witch came to him with a message. He tried to focus on it, struggling a little with the words as he made an effort to remember them.

Finn of the Salt Marsh …
Once from my arms … remember … you came,
Think of me … dream … as you whisper my name;
Remember your truce … remember the graves
Of those that still sleep in the kind sea caves.

I glanced at Kyle who had suddenly gone pale. 'Why did she say that?' he asked with a shiver. 'Why do you belong to the sea? And what did she mean by a truce? What truce? And whose graves lie in those caves?' But Finn just shrugged and didn't make much of it, as was his way.

Afterwards in order to take our mind off such things I spoke of the incredible gift of shape shifting, of changing into another being, which often enabled Finn to become that which he imagined.

In response he gave one of his familiar lop-sided grins. 'Think of it as a kind of game.'

But Kyle added eagerly, 'Can I … can we play your game?'

Finn smiled. 'It might take you half a life-time. As for me – when I go, my magic goes with me.'

That was all very well but the question I wanted to ask bubbled up inside me even though I found Finn's explanations hard to understand. 'We know that you're a master of illusion, but how does it work? How *can* you create images so real that they come alive?'

'It's a bit like walking between two worlds - dream and reality - and it only works if you allow it to,' he replied evasively. 'If you *think* it won't work, the chances are it won't. It doesn't matter what you call it: the trick is to raise a barrier between yourself and whatever touches your mind. We are all shape-shifters, we all change, but most times the shadows slip away and we don't remember them.'

I nodded as I tried to take it all in.

'But why take a path which always seems so difficult?' Kyle added.

'Because that way is *my* way,' Finn replied, and he refused to be drawn on anything more.

So we had to be content with that. However, Kyle made a few comments afterwards which were most unexpected and made me laugh.

'He rather reminds me of an *octopus* which is a bit like an alien species when you think of it—having *three* hearts. It's a solitary creature with practically no social life of its own—yet we all know how wondrously clever it is.'

I must say upon thinking about it I could see his point. But I decided not to mention this to Finn – he might not appreciate being compared to an octopus.

16

The cabin was an uncomfortable place; stifling hot in summer and bitterly cold in winter. I often lay unable to sleep listening to the wind rattling the small windows, the scream of its voice through the walls and its howls as it raced in from the sea. In the quieter times there was always the slow drip, drip of water as it found its way into cracks and crannies, and the protesting groans and sighs from the roof lifting with the draught ever so slightly.

I found myself thinking of all that had happened of late. I tried taking each day as it came, but I was filled with uneasy misgivings.

Was it really the haunting wildness and loneliness of the marsh that played upon the senses over time, causing one's imagination to run riot—or was there a more sinister and threatening role that was being played out here on this stretch of coast?

Somehow the more I thought about it, the more I found myself falling under the spell of the place and I didn't wonder that Finn had become so immersed in its magic. Neither I nor Kyle had seen much progress with the work he was carrying out in building his sea wall defences of mud and stone. We came to the conclusion that, despite his other amazing capabilities, this was largely a case of mind over matter.

I had made myself tired with all my thinking. Try as I would, I could not distance myself from the image which the mysterious and malevolent Sea Witch presented to me; an image that became stronger with time. So it was not surprising that, in such a heightened and elevated state of consciousness I slipped so easily into another world.

I was in my own body, but gifted with the ability to fly; to soar and drift, to lean on the wind and spot with an eagle's eye all that lay below. Looking down I could see the headland and the part that was Crags Head directly beneath me.

The sea was stormy, the waves surging and crashing over the rocks close to shore. Further out I caught a glimpse of a ship ploughing its way through the heavy swell. I saw flashes of white foam whipped by wind on the waves, and dolphins leaping and diving. And was that a whale's fin tail that I saw, slapping the water as it dived? I determined to drop down a little closer to take a better look.

It was all very intoxicating and surreal until the moment I realized that I was losing height. I was aware that I dreamed, but I felt the dream had a message for me and so that heightened my awareness. But I also knew that to imagine the worst always drew that fear closer, as seemed to be the way with dreams. And no sooner had the thought entered my head than the action was quick to follow.

The wind was still blowing strongly with dark, heavy ominous clouds covering the sky as I dropped lower and lower to suddenly find myself hovering above the tops of the waves. Looking down I could almost touch the crest of them, and imagined I could see the Sea Witch tearing her hair of white foam as she screamed and roared, turning into mountainous turrets as she rolled beneath me. As she raged, she seemed to reach up with greedy, grasping fingers. And although I was buffeted by winds on every side, I still managed to stay airborne just out of reach.

Then thunder crashed overhead and the roaring of the storm became louder still. Clouds of spray covered me like a shroud. Against my will I felt some force greater than I, pulling at me. I dropped lower – lower still – until there was a great splash as I suddenly hit the water and plunged beneath the waves.

I felt a moment of horror as I went down, but the moment passed. Deep under water it came as no surprise to discover that I could breathe like the many fish I saw around me. It was far from a silent world: strange sounds came to me, sounds of whistling and clicking, and of echoes that bounced to and fro.

It was a strange sensation travelling under the sea. I drifted along with no thought of my own body, as if I were being guided by some unseen hand. I passed through a cavern encrusted with shells and sea anemones where jellyfish and octopus lurked. The colours surrounding me danced in streams of rainbow light, and I saw that they were comprised of myriads of tiny jewelled fish. I was reminded of the wreck site I had visited with Finn, but I knew there were many such places far below the sea where no human had been. Many of the sea creatures I recognized; but many I did not, and among those who were strange and a little sinister was a shark who ventured inquisitively close enough in order to inspect the new intruder into its domain. Several seals pressed around me, eager to pass the word to others of my presence. And I suddenly found I had quite an audience.

Then two very strange things happened; one after the other.

Firstly, I moved some weed that hung over the entrance to the cave, and in doing so I happened to glance at what I thought might be my reflection in the water. But what I saw gave me a moment of panic.

A fleeting glance showed me a face looking up at me: Green eyes, slanted and staring. The Sea Witch …

I reeled from the shock. And then almost immediately a second strange thing happened. There came a familiar sound I could not mistake: the sound of Finn's pipe playing. It was such a comforting and welcome surprise that I did not question the absurdity of it reaching me way under the sea.

Not only did it come to me quite clearly as a message in the form of a song, but the words had particular relevance in view of the apparition I had just seen.

Beware of the depths where the whirlpools form,
Where the Sea Witch tells of the coming storm;
A storm that cuts with the sweep of her wand
Circling the depths of the space beyond;
Swim up – swim high – to the surface where
You can breathe once more the clear, sweet air;
Hurry ashore, heed well my warning,
Storms come fast between dark and dawning.

I thought of the storm already raging above, although there was no sign of its presence below. But the warning had come too late, whatever its consequences might be.

I closed my eyes in an attempt to wish myself somewhere else. And as is the way with dreams that react to danger in different ways for the worse or for the better; this time I just drifted away – like a ship running before a wind across a calm sea.

I woke as from a long sleep, to find that the storm had already died down and the sun was just starting to make silver trails across the marsh. It was the start of another day.

17

After we had hunted or fished in the early mornings and spent the day gathering roots and other edible plants for food, we often ate our meals by the fires we built at night. The evenings were a time to relax when Finn played his pipe and we talked and shared stories.

But Finn was not the only one who could tell stories. We often gathered news we had heard from radio and village talk which we thought he should know about.

'There are forests far away across the sea, the size of which you cannot imagine,' I told him. 'Think of three men standing in a circle round each with just their finger-tips touching, and you'll get some idea of the thickness of their trunks. These are giant trees that for centuries have climbed towards the sun, reaching to the heavens; and there are men who shamelessly cut them down every hour of every day.'

'A forest without these giants is as good as dead,' Kyle added. 'The loss of them will change the course of history.'

Finn was quiet … thinking. He was thinking, he told us, of all the life that would leave with each tree … all the wildlife that depended upon it.

We wondered afterwards if we should have kept this news to ourselves since it affected him so greatly. We sometimes forgot that he had very little knowledge of the outside world.

The fires we sat beside in the evenings added to our comfort but were more for cheer than warmth despite the dampening mist that rolled in from the sea.

A few days later as I sat looking into the dwindling embers of a similar blaze, the glow from within seemed to rekindle itself with dancing licks of flame. I was reminded of the fiery eyes of a creature from some fantasy world staring at me. A dragon came to mind, as had happened a few days ago. And the result of this captured my imagination in a way I could not have foreseen.

'What are you looking at, Morgan?' Finn asked.

'A dragon – or what looks like one. I can make out its eyes and long tail.'

'Oh, a dragon ... You can ride one, if you've a mind.'

I stared at him, thinking he must have lost what little common sense he had. But Kyle, who had been listening in silence, gave a sudden exclamation. '*Really.* How can we do that?'

'Wait and see,' Finn replied, getting to his feet. 'Wait and see.'

He took up his reed pipe and began to play. A shower of sparks flew up from the fire as he did so, and we saw that he began to change his shape. His arms grew and lengthened as he pitched them forward; claws suddenly appeared from his fingers. Once in a crouching position, he shook himself, displaying the reality of his now electrifying aspect. His head and body bristled with large scales which shone iridescently in the fire's glow.

The transformation caused us to rub our eyes; had we not known better we would have been terrified. The lizard-like creature gave a moaning whine which sounded like the wind as it came prowling over the marshes.

It was all so completely unexpected. This kind of thing only usually occurred when things became too tricky for Finn to tackle in the real world. Was there more than the usual quota of magic around that day?

Kyle looked at me and then took a deep breath. '*Who* was it suggested that we take a ride?'

Making wry faces at one another, we took our seats carefully on the scaly body. This alone was a scary experience as we struggled to keep hold of the creature's mane and hang on to each-other at the same time.

The sudden whoosh and jolt as we left the ground reminded me of a fairground roller coaster. The wind almost carried us off as we soared higher, and it was all we could do to keep our wits about us.

'Try not to look below!' I shouted to Kyle, but the wind snatched my words away even as I spoke.

I leaned slightly forward. Not too far, because I would soon become dizzy. What I could see as we passed over was terrain that stretched out like an endless scroll with just landmarks dotted upon it.

Kyle continued to peer below us every so often, taking hasty views of the landscape as it stretched out beneath us. We passed over Crags Head, and then continued our journey over rivers and lakes which we never knew existed before; crossing the sea where the waves rose to terrifying heights, where small ships were tossed about like flotsam, and large ones bowed low like swans before a storm.

Very soon we approached a very high mountainous region, and came upon some big birds circling there, by which I guessed they must have nests thereabouts.

The sun that had been warm in its setting, suddenly disappeared, and it became very cold. We suddenly longed to return to a more friendly familiar shore, and our dragon appeared to read our thoughts. With a dipping of its wings, it began to turn back the way we had come.

And then we saw it … a tiny black dot in the distance which grew bigger as we watched. As it drew closer we saw it was a large bird of prey, which reminded me of a vulture, although how such a creature came to be in our part of the world we had no idea.

Our dragon suddenly folded its wings and dropped. Kyle's grip on me was so tight I could hardly breathe. Although our dragon was so much bigger, it could not turn easily on account of its size, and the vulture, whose territory we must have invaded, seemed much enraged. It came at us with sharp talons and a vicious outstretched beak.

Things were not looking good. Our dragon had to be careful in a fray not to risk shaking us off. As we flew to one side we were suddenly jolted to the other. I almost lost my grip.

Grabbing his shoe, Kyle hit out at it, striking it between the eyes. He then shouted at me to feel in his pocket for some stones he had picked up, and we both sent a volley of these whistling through the air towards the angry bird. It drew back in fear emitting loud hissing sounds, and then soared above us like a great shadow, beating its wings so hard that it raised a stormy wind.

How often did we feel that all this was impossible; that none of it could be happening. It was like something from a dream. We asked few questions of Finn, but we knew there was a certain amount of magic which came and went with the moon and mist out there on the marshes.

Our journey back was without incident, and how relieved we were to see Finn quickly assume his familiar form. When we reached the cabin we found that Grandma had a cooked meal waiting for us. She always seemed to know when we would arrive and never asked any questions, likewise we never discussed things in front of her, but I suspect she already knew most things about her amazing grandson and she just nodded and smiled whenever we entered with flushed excited faces.

18

Early the following day we received a report from one of the local fishermen; there was a large leatherback turtle stranded on the beach further along the shore.

We decided to get there before the coast-guard to see if we could help. It didn't take us long to find it. Finn described the creature as 'an ancient mariner', and upon examination told us that it was getting on for one hundred years old. Lured to our shores by the rising sea temperatures, it would have swum thousands of miles to feed on the jellyfish, its favourite food.

The three of us struggled to lift it, being careful to touch only its shell, leaving its flippers free. Afterwards we watched it continuing on its journey as it dived into deeper water.

We continued walking along the beach a little further until quite by chance we came across the mouth of a tunnel leading into the open sea.

'Well I never,' Finn exclaimed. 'I never knew this was here. But I don't come round these parts often. This must have been purposely dug out at some time. I wonder what it was used for.'

I put out my hand and met the cold stone, slippery with seaweed and slime. The walls were not high but the light was enough for us to see our way, and as we went deeper the tunnel widened to reveal a cave.

Here we had another, bigger surprise.

We discovered an old fisherman in oilskins, sitting beside the skeleton of a fishing boat, smoking a pipe. He greeted us with a nod, and it seemed to us that he had either been awaiting our arrival, or he imagined we had been there all the time. Whichever the reason, he entered into conversation without further ado.

'She were once a grand old girl,' he wheezed, waving his pipe towards the boat.

'I can see that,' Finn replied warmly. 'She just got too old I suppose.'

'Too old, like me. The sea took its toll on 'er over the years. Oh aye, I knows all about what goes on in the Deep. The Sea Witch I calls 'er.'

'But that's what Finn calls her,' Kyle exclaimed. 'How strange.'

'Not strange, just fact,' the old man continued. 'She has 'er moods and ways, same as us.'

He knocked his pipe against the remaining hull of the boat, and then added, 'where do 'ee come from? Not from these parts I reckon.'

But when we told him we came from the marshes, he shook his head. 'I could tell 'ee some tales of them there marshes that 'ud scare 'ee rigid.'

We didn't quite know how to take this, so we just nodded and gave a few wry smiles. But our new acquaintance continued. 'There be hobgoblins there.'

'What's a hobgoblin?' Kyle wanted to know.

'That be a fearsome creature,' came the reply, but he didn't seem eager to offer any further explanation. Instead to our surprise he got up, shuffled over to us, and pointed in the direction from which we came.

'Now I'll show 'ee summat that'll surprise 'ee, just come along o' me.'

We all trouped out, and then had to focus everything anew as we got used to the bright sunlight. The old man pointed at a dark form along the shore, sitting on a rock.

'What do 'ee reckon that be?'

'… I think it's a boy sitting there … or maybe a girl sunbathing,' I replied.

The old man chuckled. 'A gal… well she be a gal alright.'

And then as I spoke, the figure moved.

'Wow!' Kyle exclaims, 'it's a *seal*.'

'Too right 'tis,' came the reply.' That be my gal, Pip,' our new friend explained. 'I saved 'er when she were a pup. They were goin' to kill she.'

'But why would they do that?' Kyle asked surprised.

'She were caught in their nets … they were afeard she'd tear 'em and feed on their catch. But I told 'em she were *my* gal - so I took 'er off along o' me. They didn't like it first - but now they leaves us be.'

I gave the old man one of my most brilliant smiles. 'So you looked after her when she was little, and now she's grown. What a lovely story.'

The old man then told of the close attachment that had grown between them, and how although Pip was often away for long periods at sea, she always came back to this part of the beach where she was sure of a special welcome.

Pip liked attention. The moment we were introduced she put out a flipper to shake hands, and then rolled over to have her belly rubbed. When we clapped our hands to show our appreciation, she did the same.

We were shown a few tricks she'd learnt, and laughed when she gave a loud, disgusted snort in response to the sound of a whistle; obviously something she was familiar with.

'She's almost human,' Kyle stated, once we had expressed delight at Pipe's repertoire.

But as Finn reminded us, 'she's just acting as a seal, doing the kind of things seals like to do. And since she's not held captive in any way, she's still a wild creature living her own life.'

And so it was in this way we concluded our day, sitting on the beach listening to tales told by our fisherman friend as he sat and smoked his pipe.

19

A few days later a severe gale came blowing in from the sea and brought with it a high spring tide. It was higher than any that had ever been known along that part of the coast. All thought of sea defences were swept away, as if anything so futile could do much good under normal circumstances let alone the conditions in which we now found ourselves.

The sound of water was everywhere. As it welled up from below, it gurgled and sucked; creeping sluggishly through the floorboards. Outside it surged and swirled round us in eddies, the swell lifting our wooden cabin from its supports, rocking us as if we were in a cradle.

In fact we had been set adrift, and found ourselves in a somewhat desperate situation. There was little we could do, except wait for our plight to be discovered and for help to arrive in some form or another.

Beneath us I felt the sea bucking and heaving beneath us like a beast. It was easy enough to imagine the Sea Witch mocking us, and I was sure I could hear the thunder of her voice above the rising wind. 'Think on the moon,' she seemed to say. 'Think on her tides … rise and ebb and flow.'

'There's earth magic, too,' I said aloud to remind myself and lift my spirits, but the voice I heard just dissolved into ripples of laughter that mingled with the tide.

There were many things that happened to me at that time, and I was never sure what was real and true, and what was not. I discovered that I could sometimes slip out of my body without even willing it, and I would stand on the cliff at Crags Head looking down at the sea. When I mentioned this to Kyle, he said he had similar experiences, so it must have had something to do with the strange life we led.

As I was thinking of all this, I noticed that the current had suddenly become stronger.

'Hold on!' Kyle shouted. 'Grab on to something!'

The cabin began to move faster, and we were suddenly dragged into a swirling mass of water.

'Rogue current!' Finn warned. 'We're in dead trouble now.'

'But just look,' Grandma exclaimed.

We all looked.

The water ahead of us had parted to reveal a *whale*. Could it really be a whale so far inland? Maybe it was just a very large fish. We only caught a glimpse of it, so we could have been mistaken. But a ripple seems to pass through the water from it to me, and I find myself trying to make sounds to communicate. As if in answer there come some rumbles from deep beneath the waves.

It is difficult to hear properly and the window is too small to see much. The waves are quite high. Will we all be washed out to sea and get drowned?

The wind whips up again. I try to think more clearly, but my thoughts seem to become entangled with the Sea Witch and the whale.

Is Finn really the whale? No … it's a *real* whale – or as real as I can imagine it.

Finn is close by, speaking. I can hear him quite distinctly 'She's trying to drown our world …'

Poor Finn, all his hard work – all his sea defences washed away by the Sea Witch.

And then the cabin gives a sudden big lurch. It's the whale our rescuer, pushing and thrusting us towards the shore. But what if it *isn't* the whale? I'm sure we're heading towards the land, but each time we make some progress we seem to be pushed back again out to sea. It's the Sea Witch playing cruel games.

I can see the shape of land looming up before me. Can't the others see it too? I turn to tell them the good news, but they seem to have disappeared. Perhaps they've gone into the next room to eat or take a rest.

The land comes closer and closer. And I see that it's an island - an island covered by trees. I forget about everyone and anything else, and get ready to jump ashore.

The moment my feet touch land, I'm certain of one thing: I'm a creature of Earth; I need all that it offers in the way of security. But I also have the power at times to see things others cannot, so that partly explains the puzzle for me.

The island looks so peaceful – so beautiful that I think I will stay awhile, just until the others come to join me.

20

The wind sings softly through the trees, the water sings as it laps along the beach, sea birds sing as they soar out from the land towards the open sea. The air is full of song.

What is there to dislike about it? But even as I think this, my mind begins to play me tricks.

I find a rough path and follow it, which comforts me a little, suggesting that someone – or something has passed that way before me. But I see no-one or nothing, and I soon lose track of it. The trees are not so friendly once I begin to make my way through them. They crowd together, their twisted misshapen trunks seeming to leer at me, and the under-growth grows more dense and tangled as I push my way through till at last it towers above me. The dappled sunlight seems to have disappeared.

I wish now that I had not ventured out on my own, and had waited for the others. And then I become aware that I'm not alone. Something is hidden close by, lurking, watching me. The very trees seem to turn their branches to look at me, as if I tread on forbidden ground.

I never turn to look behind me. I catch a glimpse of black shadows moving stealthily closer to me on either side, but moving so swiftly that I cannot make out what manner of things they are. I see several pairs of bright eyes peering from the undergrowth, maybe from some wild animal crouching there.

I begin to run, stumbling in my haste until my breath comes in gasps and I can go no further. The fact that whatever is there remains hidden, wishing not to show itself, makes it somehow worse – leaving me unable to face my fears.

The only sound is the wind, which tries to grab at me, as if to stop me in my tracks. Then something races past me. Not a creature or person, just another shadow. The island has become a place of shadows.

It is at this point that my mind turned to my brother, Kyle. We can often touch minds, since we think so much alike, and often our thoughts become sufficiently mingled as to become one.

Now I seem to hear his voice in the silence.

Change … We are all shape-shifters.

Could I change, I ask myself? And into *what* should I change? A fox … a raven … a snake?

I choose a raven.

Lifting myself from the ground with a rush of strong wings, I hover, my keen eyes taking in a view of the whole island. The forest looks less forbidding now.

We are all shape-changers I think, repeating the words Finn put in my mind. It's just that we lack the power to see and judge ourselves in a different way.

In this frame of mind I determine to leave the island, and make my way seawards. On my way, I scan the horizon for our floating home, but fail to see it. Instead I spy a ship, and settle myself high in the rigging. As I sway with the ship's swell, I begin to feel drowsy and my eyes close. I fight to keep them open. This is no time to sleep I tell myself. But I am weak, exhausted, and sleep soon threatens to overtake me.

And then I hear it … the sound of a reed pipe. It rises with the wind, then fades and becomes only the wind once more. But the strains of it wash over me like a healing balm.

The rocking motion of the ship becomes less, and I seem to drift down lower and lower. I can hear the murmur of the sea; it comes to me softly, whispering, closer and closer.

Then Finn is smiling at me, and I'm back in my own body again with Kyle beside me. And I can just recall Finn telling me that there is earth magic as well as sea magic. The words are familiar. I seem to recall something like that being said before.

Then he takes my hand in his, and Kyle's, so that we bond together to make a circle – a magic circle.

21

And then the tide turned again …

We were rescued at last. A rescue carried out by a team of helpers mostly fisher-folk. Work began immediately on the cabin, stripping it down, replacing the timbers, and getting it back to what it was before.

Finn seemed to have completely forgotten his former plans to preserve his part of the marsh, and concentrated instead on rebuilding his home.

Not long afterwards Kyle tried to tackle him on the subject. '… But all your work,' he faltered. 'You cannot stop now.'

'Everything has a price,' Finn answered. And we were puzzled, but had to leave it like that.

However, as things turned out the Sea Witch intended to make one final last attempt at dislodging us.

Finn had been trying to warn us in advance of those things to beware of, when the time came for us to leave him, for we had already stayed almost one season and time drew on.

'There is no such thing as a safe harbour,' he said, 'and never trust the cliff faces which over a century hide crevices and holes like sleeping snakes.' It made us think of the Crags Head which could send boulders and rocks crashing down in stormy weather.

He warned us not to let our imaginations take hold; it was all too easy to allow images to become real and take on flesh and bone when they were not intended to. We should have listened to him.

A few days later, we ventured out with the intention of digging up a few worms for bait, but the fog coming in from the sea was very thick and soon surrounded us the moment we left the safety of the cabin. We could scarcely see more than a few feet before us. It was a foolish venture, but we hated the thought of being confined for a whole day.

Wraith-like trails as high as houses marched across the marsh, blotting out the sea. The very air seemed poised ready to snatch our breath away. Everything was waiting, listening. Out of sight we heard a curlew calling, a mournful lonely wail that rose with the chill creeping up from the marsh.

Kyle pointed with a shaking finger to a figure that seemed to appear from nowhere. I looked in that direction to see a creature with a bird-like head and long black claws. But as I watched, the shape changed, pulling itself apart, and then changed once again, as a cloud changes its form.

'Do you think it's one of the Sea Witch's disguises?' Kyle asked. 'You know how clever she is.'

'But she never ventures far from the sea,' I argued in an attempt to calm him.

Kyle however, had his own opinions. 'Remember … she came before … we saw her. And her waves can attack in the form of serpents – creatures that reach out to grasp and pull people into her cauldron.'

'I know—I know—but don't think of it. You've got to block it out!'

But even as I spoke, I knew it was too late. The damage had been done.

Out from the gloom something huge was winding its way towards us, slipping in and out of the mist, writhing and coiling. It was a huge sea serpent or snake. We watched mesmerised as it flicked out its forked tongue to taste the air, licking its lips ready to locate its prey.

Then as we stood in petrified silence there was a sudden screech and we turned to find a black shape hovering. It was an eagle, one that tumbled and circled above us, then dived down, talons outstretched.

The snake, loosened from its coils, stretched upwards but the eagle was waiting for it, diving towards it, raking the air with its dagger like talons as it swooped to lift the creature up; then shaking it from side to side, sinking those sharp talons into the soft body until it fell to the ground.

Kyle and I clung together, caught up in the thrill of the moment. We watched as the snake rose once again, lashing out desperately, although wounded, grasping at the eagle as it hovered dangerously close. Then with one last mighty grab the snake caught hold, twining itself quickly round the eagle's body and squeezing it. The eagle thrashed its wings as hard as it could in its attempts to free itself, turning its head round at all angles to get a stronger grip. But the snake wriggled out from it, winding, twisting and coiling, so that the eagle's plight looked seemingly hopeless.

And then Kyle did a brave thing.

He rushed out and hacked at the snake with the old rake he carried, the one we used to unearth worms for bait. With one mighty heave he managed to cut it in two.

The pieces fell apart and melted into the mist. And suddenly there was a loud screaming overhead, not from the eagle, but from several gulls battling against the wind which had suddenly whipped up.

And the spell was broken. We clapped our hands to our ears and drew deep breaths.

Finn stood there shaking his head but wearing that attractive lopsided grin we had come to know so well.

'Thank you Kyle,' he said. 'You saved me that time – only just don't go throwing bad thoughts around like that anymore on foggy days like this.'

22

It had been early spring when we first came to stay at the cabin. But now summer had come and gone, rapidly changing to autumn as the days shortened. The many shades of green on the marsh now turned to gold, purple and red.
A most beautiful time to appreciate the wetlands, but we knew that our time there was fast coming to a close.

As Finn said, nothing lasts forever. And I knew he had given us something better than we could have ever hoped for in view of the future. We need never be afraid of anything that life might throw at us if only we could face up to our worst fears. We had suddenly grown years older.

We often wandered about the marsh for days, noting the wildlife that lived there. Apart from the many birds there were waterfowl, frogs, butterflies and many rare plants. And how we savoured those times; there was often only the sound of the sea birds, the distant murmur of waves and wind. But there was also a special tang to the air that came across the marshes, different to that of the harbour with its fish and seaweed scents we had been used to; the grasses, the sky and air were like nothing I could find words for.

When we were out working at something, Finn would steal quietly up to us, like a shadow, his thoughts often coming to us as lightly as a breath of wind.

I would glance at him in the familiar way I had come to view him in those days, as he brushed the wispy hair from his eyes, and grinned at us with the dimple that appeared in his cheek every so often when he smiled. He used his hands to express himself which always made his narrative more exciting as he spoke, often plucking at a stalk of grass from where he sat, placing it in his mouth and chewing on it.

His words in answer to my unspoken wish to help dispel that anger and sadness I sensed within him, left a cold shiver down my spine. All he would say was, "time is running out".

Then I would try to imagine the Sea Witch as I had last caught a glimpse of her on the marsh that day, but I found the picture in my mind had changed. This time I saw her as pale and yellow-haired as a mermaid with a smile that held enchantment, her eyes deep blue like that of the ocean. It was difficult to remind myself of her other self; one who could bewitch and yet suck the life from one according to her mood.

Finn told us of the continual wars of land and sea; and I thought of the times when the land seemed to be fighting back, causing deep chasms and ridges to appear with eruptions far beneath the earth. But this only made the Sea Witch angry; she would send monstrous waves to rise that submerged and drowned whole islands. She had never been a friend to man.

Finn had warned us so many times: "If she can, she will take you … as she has taken so many - to join those who live with her below the waves. She takes all those she can who are land bound. There are vast chambers below the waves where things are hidden of which man has no knowledge. The moon also has her part to play and in days long past, men made sacrifices to both."

Of course all this made us think about things much differently from the way we saw them at the beginning. But it wasn't quite the end of the story. There was still one card left to play, and that belonged to Finn.

23

One day something happened to change every-thing. It began like any other, going about our usual duties taking turns fishing along the shore or foraging inland.

Being so engrossed we didn't notice the approach of the two men with a dog. They very briefly introduced themselves as coastguards, although that was open to suspect. They seemed vaguely familiar, and I was reminded of the incident shortly after we'd arrived when Kyle had been kidnapped.

'What d'you want?' Finn asked, in a tone of voice which suggested he already knew.

'Just a few words, mate. Won't take long … Shall we go inside?' he asked, 'Out o' sight and hearing o' these young 'uns.'

'Just as you like,' Finn replied gruffly, and the door of the cabin slammed shut behind them.

The dog was left outside, guarding the place, or so it appeared.

Kyle and I looked at each other without saying a word. We knew it was not good.

The voices inside the cabin were raised slightly, and we could hear a lot of argument going on.

At last I turned to Kyle, and said, 'Remember Carys? Remember how they got on to her … but Finn is out here away from everybody. What harm is he doing to anyone?'

'Where's Grandma?' Kyle asked. 'I bet she'd give them a piece of her mind.'

Before I could answer the door opened and one of the men came out. He nodded to us, and then walked over out of the wind to light his pipe. We waited expectantly and after a few minutes he decided to speak a few words.

'Nothing to worry about; I think your friend might be considering comin' along o' us shortly, just for a few hours like.'

'Finn won't like–'Kyle began, but I shook my head quickly to silence him. It would do no good trying to cause more trouble by interfering.

But Kyle was keen to put in a word or two.

'Whatever it is,' he reasoned, 'he never meant to cause any trouble.'

'Huh,' the man replied. 'He's always doin' *that* one way or t' other.'

The wind along the coast was constant and chill, a fine mist slapping our garments against our bodies. It seemed a long time before the cabin door opened again, and the second man stepped out.

He motioned our man over and they spoke in low voices together, but I heard a little, and understood that Finn was in the process of saying a few words to Grandma and collecting some things he wanted to take with him before joining them.

'What do we do now?' Kyle asked me, and I shrugged.

'Nothing we can do; nothing but watch and wait. The choice is up to Finn now.'

The men stamped about, kicking up bits of mud and stones, growing more and more impatient, while the dog ambled around sniffing for anything interesting on the ground.

Time seemed to drag. There was no sign of the door opening, and at last one of them went and banged upon it, shouting for Finn to come out.

'What's goin' on there?' he hollered.

Grandma appeared at the door, wiping her

hands calmly on her apron. 'No-one here,' she announced. 'Come and see.'

The men went in and looked round, shoving things out of the way, knocking everything around while Grandma shouted at them. We could hear them swearing and muttering loudly among themselves.

'Where be the rascal?'

'You tell me. Nowhere for he to go - nowhere but miles of blessed marsh from 'ere to harbour - some twenty miles back.'

I looked at Kyle and grinned. We hoped this might be a good sign.

But suddenly there came a great roar from the cabin and someone was pounding loudly on the window.

'Look Jake! Will 'ee just look out there!'

Kyle and I looked where the man was pointing out at sea. We could see a shape there, a form that was getting smaller as we watched. We raced quickly towards the edge of the marsh with the two men following.

Finn it was, and we could only just see him against the sunlit waves. There was a mist coming in from the sea in long drifts, and we watched until we could no longer see him through the haze.

'Well, I'll be blessed; what does the beggar think he'll be able to do out that far … swim for it?'

'Quick, get that old boat there and let's go look for the blighter,' they cried.

And that's what they did; trawling back and fore in Finn's little boat for several hours. But they didn't find him. There was nothing out there but ocean.

Grandma seemed none the wiser. If she knew anything, she wasn't telling. Just nodded her head at our many questions and went on about her work.

We talked it over, trying to make sense of it.

'Magic such as he used would make little of distance,' Kyle reasoned. 'He could easily have dodged them … '

'But instead he chose another way – a way only he could and would take.' It amazed me that I could speak the words so flatly without showing too much emotion.

'Wait until tomorrow,' I told Kyle, hoping that a new day would reawaken some new hope.

……

That night a great storm arose. It lasted for three days. Mountainous waves again lashed the shore and ran inland over the marshes; then there was a lull and the wind dropped. And at low tide a miracle was discovered.

A causeway had appeared - consisting of many stones which could only have been thrown up by the waves. It followed a straight line, partly covered by water and extending as far as the eye could see, stretching all the way to the crag on which the old monastery once stood; a barrier reaching up to the level of the surrounding marsh and thus preventing the tide flowing through.

Where did it come from? How did it form so quickly in so short a time? No-one knew.

But we thought *we* did. It was something Finn had always wanted: a link opening up a path to the land stolen by the Sea Witch – land which she eventually gave back to him. His stories were all around us wherever we went, as if every step we took had a special meaning. I wish now that I'd taken more notice of them in the days that came after. I thought they would stay in my head; but age and time rubs away so much in the end. That's why I made some notes, so I shouldn't forget.

There will always be the war between the land and sea, and Finn was part of that war - as are we all. We *can* do something about the sea taking our land – our world. But we have to give something back, as Finn did. I often asked myself if it was worth it in the end, but the answer always came back the same: *The worth is in the act.* And I knew it to be true.

We waited for him to return. We waited a long time. But he never came back … at least not until … But that's another story.

We knew the Sea Witch had taken him. It was her part of the bargain. And although she continued to flood inland further along the coast, she left Finn's part alone.

Yet now and again when the nights are very quiet and still, we often think we hear the sound of his pipe playing somewhere across the sea.